The DBT Workbook for Alcohol and Drug Addiction

of related interest

Help! I'm Addicted
A Trans Girl's Self-Discovery and Recovery
Rhyannon Styles
ISBN 978 1 78775 658 8
eISBN 978 1 78775 659 5

Living at the Speed of Light
Navigating Life with Bipolar Disorder, from Depression
to Mania and Everything in Between
Katie Conibear
Foreword by Calum Harris, Lorraine Gillies and Aditya Sharma
ISBN 978 1 78775 557 4
eISBN 978 1 78775 558 1

What I Do to Get Through
How to Run, Swim, Cycle, Sew, or Sing Your Way Through Depression
Edited by Olivia Sagan and James Withey
Foreword by Cathy Rentzenbrink
ISBN 978 1 78775 298 6
eISBN 978 1 78775 299 3

Confronting Shame
How to Understand Your Shame and Gain Inner Freedom
Ilse Sand
ISBN 978 1 83997 140 2
eISBN 978 1 83997 141 9

The DBT Workbook for Alcohol and Drug Addiction

Skills and Strategies for Emotional Regulation, Recovery, and Relapse Prevention

Laura J. Petracek, PhD, LCSW

Foreword by Gillian Galen, PsyD

Jessica Kingsley Publishers
London and Philadelphia

First published in Great Britain in 2023 by Jessica Kingsley Publishers
An imprint of Hodder & Stoughton Ltd
An Hachette Company

I

Copyright © Laura J. Petracek 2023
Foreword Copyright © Gillian Galen 2023

The activity on pp.160–162, Diary card, is reproduced with
kind permission from Dr Keith Sutton.

A CIP catalogue record for this title is available from the
British Library and the Library of Congress

ISBN 978 1 83997 252 2
eISBN 978 1 83997 251 5

Printed and bound in the United States by Integrated Books International

Jessica Kingsley Publishers' policy is to use papers that are natural, renewable and recyclable
products and made from wood grown in sustainable forests. The logging and manufacturing
processes are expected to conform to the environmental regulations of the country of origin.

Jessica Kingsley Publishers
Carmelite House
50 Victoria Embankment
London EC4Y 0DZ UK

www.jkp.com

For Snigdha and David

Contents

Foreword

GILLIAN GALEN, PSYD

When I first came to Dialectical Behavioral Therapy (DBT) I was fascinated by the concept of dialectics. I guess I had never really thought about this idea that two opposing things could be true at the same time. It seems so obvious now—of course there are multiple truths and multiple and opposing positions or perspectives that can be true at the same time. Well, I can say this now after more than 15 years of doing DBT! Thinking dialectically is not always easy and something that I would challenge you to work on, as there is freedom in simply being able to acknowledge the multiple perspectives around us. If you are not sure about this, you will see that this workbook is the perfect example of dialectical thinking! Think about it this way—AA/NA can both be exactly what you need to find and maintain sobriety, and also cannot be enough to find and maintain sobriety. Ask yourself—can both of these statements be true?

If you are reading this book, you probably know that addiction and mental illness both have the powerful ability to consume and take over your life. Alcohol, drugs, and strong uncontrolled emotions can shut down your mind, color your thinking, change your behavior, destroy your relationships, and profoundly impact the decisions you make. So how can you change your path? Many people use the wisdom and support of AA/NA to navigate toward and maintain sobriety, but, as Dr Petracek found along her own journey, AA/NA, while instrumental for sobriety, was simply not enough to manage the strong emotions that began to consume her life. In an effort to destigmatize mental illness and addiction, Dr Petracek courageously shares her own journey through addiction and bipolar disorder, and her discovery that neither AA/NA nor DBT alone was sufficient, but instead a synthesis of the two proved to be the intervention she was looking for. She created this unique and powerful workbook to share that wisdom with us. If AA/NA is the roadmap to maintaining sobriety, DBT provides an overlay of skills to stay present, tolerate pain, regulate emotions, and take care of your relationships, skills you will need to successfully work the Twelve Steps. This seems like a beautiful dialectical synthesis to me. Dr Petracek was absolutely right when she said it is "time for a more complex approach."

In this groundbreaking workbook, Dr Petracek has created a power dialectical synthesis; she has taken two perspectives, AA/NA and DBT, and created a new roadmap to manage addiction and your emotions. She has approached two different worlds and demonstrated how you can, in fact, use both to support your sobriety. Dr Petracek takes the fundamental DBT skills of mindfulness, interpersonal effectiveness, emotion regulation, and distress tolerance, and expertly teaches the reader how to practice the skills and how each skill directly supports the working of the Steps.

It both surprises me and it does not (a dialectic) that this book was not written long ago. It makes so much sense and fills a huge gap for those who struggle with both addiction and mental illness. Dr Petracek's guidance is strong and steady as she enhances your working the Steps with the most important DBT skills to increase your awareness, decrease your judgments, improve, repair, and maintain your relationships, learn about and regulate your emotions, increase your capacity to tolerate distress in a new way, find compassion for yourself, and accept reality, especially when it is painful. This workbook is a wonderful example of challenging two worlds, AA/NA and DBT, to pay attention to their powerful ability to complement one another.

If you are reading this book, I applaud you for your openness and curiosity about something new. With Dr Petracek's clinical expertise and lived experience you have an expert guide to lead you through an enhanced and skills-based journey to work the Twelve Steps. This workbook brings you on a path towards strengthening your awareness and control over your sobriety and emotions, and even more it will be a beacon to building a life worth living.

I expect this will be a deeply valuable resource to all who embark on this journey, and to both the AA/NA and DBT communities for years to come. Thank you, Dr Petracek, for this invaluable contribution.

Gillian Galen, PsyD
Psychology Instructor, Harvard Medical School,
Author of DBT for Dummies (*John Wiley & Sons, 2021*)

Part 1

Introduction

Pain is Inevitable; Suffering is Optional

In 1979, just shy of three years sober, my emotions began to unravel. I put deposits on three separate apartments. My thoughts spiraled out of control and were not coherent to the people around me. People at AA suggested I attend more meetings, work another Step, or sponsor more people. I understood they meant well and I took their suggestions, but still sank deeper into despair. I became more and more depressed. I woke up early every morning, sobbing.

I was very fortunate to have sober women in my life, including my sponsor, who lovingly and without judgment encouraged me to seek outside help. Feeling suicidal and hopeless, I finally called my sponsor at 3am; she brought me to a safe place—a local rehab. Being clean and sober, I didn't want to go to a psychiatric ward. I was afraid: what if I was both "crazy" and an alcoholic?

After taking a series of psychological tests, the psychiatrist diagnosed me with manic depressive illness (which today is called bipolar disorder). At first, I was resistant to taking medication because I had heard it said in the rooms of AA that taking medication does not qualify as being sober. However, I agreed to accept that medication could help me. The psychiatrist started me on lithium, which helped to reduce symptoms of mania and alleviate my depression.

More than 30 years later, I experienced harassment and bullying in my job. This coincided with my only daughter leaving for college that fall. I fell into deep despair. Soon after, my therapist of seven-and-a-half years told me over the phone, "I am thinking of terminating you." During my next session, they did. That was the last straw. My psychiatrist suggested a new treatment for my depression. Unfortunately, it backfired and triggered my mania. Despite the increased dosage of lithium, I still struggled. Finally, my psychiatrist suggested attending an intensive Dialectical Behavior Therapy skills group. Dialectical Behavior Therapy, or DBT, is a skills-based approach comprised of four different modules.[1] Could DBT help with my intense, painful emotions, including my quality of recovery?

I have successfully worked in psychology and social work for over 30 years while managing my mental health and sobriety. Nobody should feel shame or self-loathing discussing mental health struggles. Unfortunately, in our society, and even in AA/NA, there is still a stigma about depression, anxiety, and mental health issues. While the Twelve Steps help the alcoholic achieve and maintain sobriety and help the addict get clean, there is little in the AA/NA literature that offers additional tools to alleviate mental distress.

Within the spirit of transparency and destigmatization, my main goal in writing this book was to provide a resource for people in recovery who struggle with emotional dysregulation. The DBT skills outlined in these pages can help people who suffer from mental health issues as well as addiction, especially those with depression, anxiety, post-traumatic stress disorder (PTSD), and complex trauma.

The simultaneous embrace of acceptance and change in DBT is consistent with the philosophical approach found in Twelve-Step programs, expressed in the serenity prayer: "God, grant me the serenity to accept the things I cannot change, the courage to change the things I can, and the wisdom to know the difference."

When I heard the quote "pain is inevitable; suffering is optional" during a DBT group, a light went off in my head. I've heard this saying many times in AA/NA meetings over the years, but the *how* to not suffer always eluded me. Although pain is part of life, it is focusing on that pain that causes suffering. Our thoughts and perceptions about the situation also cause suffering. Unfortunate events, problems, and disappointments are like arrows that cause pain. For example, suffering may be self-deprecating thoughts, self-blame, or getting down on yourself.

Learning and applying Radical Acceptance (for example, stop fighting reality) and DBT skills have changed how I relate to my thoughts and emotions, which has helped reduce my suffering greatly. I am so grateful. Having struggled with depression and mental illness most of my life, acceptance is a form of self-compassion. Before attending the DBT program, I had little self-compassion. Now, I have a photo of myself as a child on my nightstand. When I find myself having unkind or judgmental thoughts about myself (awareness is half the battle), I say loving words to her, and it helps me course-correct. Don't believe everything you think!

Time for a more complex approach
Dr Bob and Bill W. created the Twelve Steps of Alcoholic/Addicts Anonymous (AA) to establish guidelines for the best way to overcome alcohol addiction.

The Twelve Steps and the *Big Book* are considered the blueprint for recovery and the core of AA/NA that's helped people recover for over 80 years. Bill W.'s experience in psychotherapy had a profound impact on his understanding of recovery and Step work. After his own experience with severe depression, he suggested applying psychotherapy to AA/NA principles.

Individuals in AA/NA who have both psychological and substance abuse problems sometimes overlook their psychological difficulties and attribute their anxiety or depression to previous drug and alcohol use. Combining the application of DBT and the Twelve Steps, this workbook allows individuals to address the underlying issues of addiction and managing daily stressors. This combination helps build relationships in life to develop and maintain a healthy state of mind while maintaining the daily commitment to stay sober. This book assumes some familiarity with the Twelve Steps, but for more information on these please refer to *Twelve Steps and Twelve Traditions*.

The activities are designed to simplify and demystify DBT concepts, such as mindfulness, interpersonal effectiveness, emotion regulation, and distress tolerance. I hope you will find this workbook helpful on your recovery journey towards a life worth living and a life beyond your wildest dreams!

Dialectical Behavioral Therapy Explained

Dialectical Behavioral Therapy (DBT) is a combination of cognitive, behavioral, and mindfulness therapy. The goal of DBT is to change negative thinking patterns and destructive behaviors into ones with positive outcomes. DBT effectively helps people regulate their emotions, build self-management skills, and reduce anxiety and stress. DBT is a research-based way to establish coping mechanisms to implement in environments that may elicit old, destructive substance abuse patterns.

How did DBT begin?

In the late 1980s, Dr Marsha Linehan, Professor of Psychology at the University of Washington, founded the Linehan Institute and developed DBT with her colleagues. She and her team discovered that Cognitive Behavioral Therapy (CBT) alone did not work as well as expected in patients with borderline personality disorder (BPD). So, they added mindfulness, interpersonal effectiveness, and emotion regulation, to develop a treatment that would meet these patients' unique needs. As a result, DBT helps people experiencing suicidal thoughts and difficulty managing emotions.[2]

Research has shown success in applying DBT to people suffering from substance use disorder.[3] DBT helps clients establish coping mechanisms to reduce anxiety in situations that elicit the stress response associated with alcohol and substance abuse. Anxiety levels increase when people recovering are in environments that trigger old responses. DBT can help people in recovery shift negative and impulsive thinking into positive self-talk and mindful behaviors. The four modules of DBT are mindfulness, interpersonal effectiveness, emotion regulation, and distress tolerance.

1. Mindfulness

Mindfulness skills include being in touch with self and others, and furthering acceptance of self and others. In this first module, you'll learn mindfulness skills to help you gain awareness. One way of becoming aware of yourself is to remain present in the moment and to focus on your immediate feelings, thoughts, and behaviors. It's essential to learn mindfulness skills because many alcoholics and addicts are impulsive and triggered quickly. The mindfulness module offers skills to reduce impulsive behavior, which is a critical aspect of recovery.

Mindfulness skills play a central role in DBT. All subsequent DBT emotion regulation skills hinge on being able to practice mindfulness. Mindfulness's primary function is to reduce emotional sensitivity and regulate emotions.

Mindfulness refers to bringing one's attention to the here and now. Mindfulness is when you realize your thoughts are "somewhere else," and return to your breath. It involves recognizing and observing your feelings. Like shining a warm, soft light, it is compassionate and nonjudgmental. By being in the here and now, you can attend to thoughts, feelings, and behaviors without emotional dysregulation. Mindfulness is a valuable tool that helps you make thoughtful decisions.

By not accepting your experiences, making rash decisions, and forming assumptions, you end up living a life full of misery. Attempting to suppress your emotional responses only makes matters worse. Moreover, the longer you try to deny these feelings, the more they gain intensity. Mindfulness helps break the cycle of dysregulation and reduces misery.

Mindfully experiencing emotions means observing what comes up. Observe them, feel them, and try not to suppress them. As a result, our emotional experiences are less upsetting and pass quickly. Permitting them to be there lets emotions take their natural course as fleeting, changing, and transitional.

2. Interpersonal effectiveness

This module of DBT teaches interpersonal effectiveness skills, meaning honest and effective communication. People in recovery may be sensitive to absolute or imagined rejection. Frustrations due to feeling rejected strain interpersonal relationships, and sometimes the alcoholic or addict thinks the only thing to do is pick up a drink or a drug. Interpersonal effectiveness will help you define your boundaries, exhibit more assertiveness, and manage conflict in a healthy way.

Interpersonal effectiveness, at its most basic, refers to the ability to interact with others.[4] DBT skills are an enhancement to Twelve-Step recovery because the way we communicate affects our relationships. The quality of our relationships influences our wellbeing, our sense of self-esteem, our self-confidence, and our very understanding of who we are.

This module includes the following skills:

- Attending to relationships
- Balancing priorities versus demands
- Balancing our "wants" with our "shoulds"
- Cultivating awareness of mastery and self-respect.

There are many skills in the Twelve-Step literature related to communication and interaction with others. Two critical components of interpersonal effectiveness are asking for things and saying "no" to requests when appropriate. Factors to consider when asking for something or saying "no" are:

- *Priorities:* Very important? Increase the intensity of asking or saying "no."
- *Relationship:* Weak, tenuous, fragile, injured? Consider reducing the intensity of asking or saying "no."
- *Self-respect:* On the line? Increase the intensity of asking or saying "no."

Gaining objective effectiveness

Objective effectiveness is the measure of how close you came to achieving the goal of the interaction. It helps you understand the difference between balancing what is important to you and what is important to others, that is, your priorities vs. people's demands. Objective effectiveness is key to setting clear boundaries and finding a balance. This distinction can make it easier to say "no," to ask for help when you need it, and to offer help when you can.

Maintaining relationships

If you don't do a regular inventory of your relationships, this can create stress and emotional vulnerability. DBT skills and the Twelve Steps teach relationship skills to help you navigate through conflicts.

While maintaining relationships with others is a main priority, we need to understand how important the particular connection is to us, how we want the person to feel about us, and what we need to do to keep the relationship going. Alcoholics and addicts can also use interpersonal effectiveness skills in their relationship with themselves.

When working toward an objective, it's essential to clarify what we want from the interaction and to identify what we need to do to get the results. For example, when our goal is to keep our self-respect, we will use interpersonal skills to help us feel how we would like to feel after the interaction is over, and to stick to our values and to the truth.

Building mastery and self-respect

It is essential to act in a way that is in accordance with your values. One way to build self-respect is to stand up for yourself, assertively express your opinions, and listen to your intuition; as the AA/NA program requests of us: "Do the next right thing."

3. Emotion regulation

Lack of emotional regulation is the primary trigger in alcohol and drug relapse. In this module of DBT, you'll learn to detect, comprehend, and handle your emotions better.

This module focuses on understanding the source of our emotions and reactions and applying specific skills to manage them instead of being controlled by them. These skills focus on lessening our vulnerability to negative emotions and reframing them as positive emotional experiences. In this module, we take it skill-by-skill to strengthen your foundation of emotional intelligence to tackle and handle painful feelings and to help foster positive ones.

Emotion regulation skills include:

- Letting things go
- Wearing the world like a loose garment
- Incorporating positivity into our lives.

Some of our experiences of negative emotions lead to spiraling out of control. Therefore, learning to manage and regulate emotions is a core part of DBT and working the Twelve Steps.

Primary and secondary emotions

There are primary and secondary emotions. Primary emotions are spontaneous reactions to external factors—anger, sorrow, joy, fear, disgust, guilt/shame, interest, surprise. Secondary emotions are emotional reactions we have to other emotions.

For example, a person might feel ashamed as a result of feeling anxious. In this case, anxiety is the primary emotion while shame is the secondary emotion. When my dog Ruffles died, I felt tremendous grief. That was my primary emotion. Feeling lonely was my secondary emotion.

Differentiating between primary and secondary emotions

- Is this emotion a direct reaction to an external event? *Primary.*
- Is the emotion becoming more intense over time? *Secondary.*
- Do you experience the emotion more frequently than the events that prompted the emotion? *Secondary.*
- Does the emotion continue long after the event, interfere with your abilities in the present, and affect new and different experiences? *Secondary.*

As noted by neuroscientist Jill Bolte-Taylor, the average emotion and physiological lifespan is a mere 90 seconds.[5] Most people are surprised to learn this. Sometimes when we're triggered, either internally or externally, several factors affect our feelings: the cues in the environment, our thoughts, our beliefs, and our physiological sensations. Some of this is hard-wired, and some of it depends on our history.

4. Distress tolerance

At some point in our recovery, we have to cope with pain and distress. Our pain can feel overwhelming at times. When we're in emotional pain, the dimensions of time disappear. There are two types of distress tolerance skills: *crisis survival skills* involve learning how to ride out an overwhelming situation and; *reality acceptance* which helps us reduce misery and suffering by accepting life as it is.[6] One of the biggest challenges in recovery is learning how to not act on these urges, thereby avoiding a potential relapse.

Crisis survival skills help the alcoholic or addict navigate through a challenging situation without making it worse. Here are some examples of crisis survival skills:

- Leaving the situation
- Distracting yourself with activities
- Self-soothing behaviors
- Thinking it through, imagining you did pick up a drink or a drug
- Breathing and muscle relaxation.

Reality acceptance skills help you out of suffering by accepting things as they are. When we fight the reality of a situation, we only make it worse. Denial is one of the most common defense mechanisms of alcoholics and addicts.

Reality acceptance skills can prolong the mastery of "pause" found in AA/NA. Here are some examples of reality acceptance skills:

- *Turning the mind:* This helps distract yourself and deal with painful psychological realities without avoidance.
- *Willingness:* In DBT, willingness refers to recognizing the reality of the situation and being an effective problem-solver. It is the opposite of fighting what is happening and refusing to tolerate the facts around you.[7] It is similar to the HOW skill—Honesty, Open-mindedness, and Willingness.
- *Half-smile:* In DBT, there is a practice called "half-smile." When you are feeling down, sad, annoyed, upset, bored, or depressed, make the effort of a half-smile. It helps neutralize the possible escalation of these feelings.
- *Willing hands:* This is a DBT concept to let go and move on. Your open hands are letting go of the pain you could otherwise be holding on to, and you're allowing yourself to move forward without being weighed down by painful past events.[8]

Similarities between AA/NA and DBT

AA/NA	DBT
You never complete the Steps—once you have gone through them, you go through them again	You go through the skills, then you repeat them, again and again—practice, practice, practice
Recovery is a lifelong process; there is no cure for alcoholism or addiction—it can only be arrested	Practicing skills is a lifelong process to achieve and maintain a life worth living
Relapse is common, but the longer you are in recovery, the less likely you are to relapse	A relapse of old behavior is expected, but the longer you practice the skills, the less likely you are to revert to the old behavior
For each problem, there is a Step/s or Principle/s	For each situation, there is a skill/are skills
All that is required is a desire to stop drinking or using	All that is needed is a desire to want a life worth living

Core Concepts of DBT and the Twelve Steps

Throughout the book, the four modules of DBT are used in combination with each of the Twelve Steps. DBT is a skills-based approach and includes four different stages.[9] To achieve the goals in Stages 1–4, you'll need the skills found in the four modules of DBT: mindfulness, interpersonal effectiveness, emotion regulation, and distress tolerance.

The focus of DBT is to create a dialectical lifestyle that reflects balanced behavioral patterns: balanced actions, balanced emotions, and balanced cognition.[10] When something is dialectical it means that there are two opposing forces, feelings, or situations that happen simultaneously. For example, "It is raining, *and* the sun is shining through." Another dialectic is, "Quarantine was brutal, *and* we got through the crisis." By thinking and acting dialectically, you can keep your emotions calm *and* look through a new lens to see two truths in a situation.

Similarly, the dialectic of the Twelve Steps is to realize the challenges of sobriety *and* that you can overcome them by living a disciplined life with honesty, hope, and integrity.

Both DBT and AA/NA emphasize abstinence as the ultimate goal of treatment. Both treatments underscore the importance of building a supportive, clean, and sober community.[11] Both DBT and the Twelve Steps focus on behavior change, developing sober interests, and identifying and changing dysfunctional thoughts and behavior.[12]

Both AA and NA literature focuses on 12 principles as guiding values that help you successfully work through each Step. These are the core values that your daily life needs—not just to reach a state of sobriety, but also to actively maintain it. Make these values yours, and incorporate them into your recovery.

Comparison of concepts: DBT and the Twelve Steps

DBT	TWELVE STEPS
Emotional dysregulation	Emotional unmanageability
Having emotions that are overly intense in comparison to the situation that triggered them. It means not being able to calm down, avoiding emotions because you feel them too strongly, or being unable to switch your focus from the negative	When you have no control over how you are going to feel or react at any particular time
Interpersonal conflict	Toxic relationships
A person may go back and forth between love and hate in close relationships. Relationships may be stormy. There may be deep fear of abandonment and frantic efforts to avoid losing connection	A toxic relationship is characterized by insecurity, self-centeredness, dominance, and control. A toxic relationship is dysfunctional
Self-invalidation	Spiritual bankruptcy
The inability to maintain one or more major components of identity	Feeling an empty hole inside, being out of touch with your sponsor, being judgmental, not attending AA/NA meetings
Behavioral problems	Self-will run riot
Easily getting annoyed or nervous. Often appearing angry. Putting blame on others	Living a life driven by self-will with no thought for anyone else. An alcoholic or addict is an example of self-will run riot in itself, but it's really the mindset that drives this spiral
Cognitive distortions	Stinking thinking
Irrational thoughts that can influence your emotions	A term used in Twelve-Step groups to describe someone who is engaged in negative thoughts that could lead to destructive behavior

We have compared these two modalities and now understand the parallels between them. We can also look at the Twelve Steps through the lens of DBT to understand the gaps, and how these frameworks enhance one another, resulting in a new hybrid framework that is accessible to you and others in recovery.

Putting it all together

You now have a better understanding of DBT and how to apply its principles to the Twelve Steps of AA/NA. Applying DBT to the Twelve Steps is a valuable addition to your recovery program by helping reduce symptoms of emotional distress and diminish the urge to pick up a drink or a drug. If you find yourself in emotional pain and want to learn some new coping strategies, this workbook is written just for you.

Each of the Twelve Steps is broken down in-depth along with the corresponding DBT skills. Working through this workbook is a commitment to yourself to do the activities and put your new skills into practice. I'm excited for you to take the first step by beginning the next chapter.

The activities marked with ⊛ can be downloaded from https://library.jkp.com/redeem using the code DCUQDTP

Part 2

The Twelve Steps and DBT

Chapter 1

Step One: I Can't Stop...

In this chapter:
- → Stage 1 of DBT
  - – Activity: The alcoholic/addict psyche vs. dry drunk syndrome
- → Radical Acceptance
  - – Activity: Radical Acceptance skills
- → The sober self
  - – Activity: Dry drunk syndrome vs. the sober self
  - – Activity: Create an action plan to stay abstinent today
- → Community reinforcement strategies combining DBT and the Twelve Steps
  - – Activity: Reinforcing clean and sober behaviors
- → Healthy contrarianism
  - – Activity: Developing a plan for healthy contrarianism

Step One	The DBT translation
Step One is about powerlessness and unmanageability	We practice Radical Acceptance that we are powerless over alcohol and drugs that caused our lives to become unmanageable

Today, I am in recovery for both alcoholism and bipolar disorder, but never cured. I attend therapy to treat my bipolar disorder and other issues, and attend AA for alcoholism/addiction.

I come from a family and extended family pickled with alcoholism and mental illness. I often felt despair growing up. When I was 13, I had my first drink. After that, I began self-medicating symptoms of neglect, verbal abuse, and depression. My drinking and drug career were a short, but intense, four years between the ages of 13 and 17, before I crashed and burned.

At age 14, I started drinking every weekend with friends and smoking pot every day. When I got my driver's license, that's when my disease took off. I started each day smoking pot, then getting high at school, getting high at the fast-food job I worked at, and drinking afterward. I didn't sleep much. I burned the candle at both ends in my addiction. A friend turned me on to white cross (an amphetamine). Soon I was drinking a case of beer every day, getting high, and still managing to get straight A's. However, I started to hear the phone ringing at all hours and became paranoid. I decided to cut down on taking speed, but my depression worsened. Also, I started feeling attracted to girls and felt ashamed and alone. I used alcohol and drugs to cope with the stress of pretending I was straight and to numb my sexual feelings. I'd wake up every morning depressed, sit at the kitchen table, and cry.

Rightly worried, my mother asked what she could do. I said I didn't know. She made an appointment with a psychiatrist. I felt so ashamed I laid on the bottom of the back car seat, fearing someone might see me going to the appointment. At the psychiatrist's, he reflected that he heard and saw that I was very depressed. He prescribed an antidepressant. I started taking it and felt a little bit better, but I also started feeling suicidal.

At this point, I was drowning in hopelessness and despair. I prayed to God, as I often did. My prayer was simple: "Help me." I went into my parents' medicine cabinet and took the sleeping pills to my bedroom. I laid them out, one by one. I didn't want to freak out if I took a bunch of them at once. I blacked out. My mother knew something was wrong. She looked through my room and found the empty pill bottles in my dresser drawer. She immediately called an ambulance. On the way to the hospital, I flatlined. I was dead on arrival. I was in a coma for a week. When I came out of the coma, I again felt fear and despair, as I had no tools at my disposal for living.

Now what was I going to do? They admitted me to an adolescent psychiatric ward. Lucky for me, although the year was 1974, the adolescent psych ward in Minneapolis was progressive, client-centered, and did a chemical dependency assessment. My counselor told me she thought I was chemically dependent. She asked if I'd like to talk to someone in AA. I said, "Sure." A woman from AA came to the psychiatric ward and spent over an hour with me. "I don't think you're crazy; I think you're an alcoholic."

"Really?" I felt some relief: one, that I was not "crazy" (although I doubted this), and two, comfort that I wouldn't have to go back home. The woman from AA asked why I didn't want to go. "I'm afraid if I go home, I'll try to commit suicide again—but this time I'll succeed." However, my parents had concerns about the rehab facilities in our area after checking them out, stating they were "sketchy," and wanted to make sure I was safe. The woman from AA suggested a new option. "I can help you with the process to get emancipated as a minor. After that, you're considered an adult by the court and can sign yourself in for treatment." As soon as I was ready to leave the psych ward, she helped me find a rehab just for teenagers. A short time later, when my parents came to visit, they saw that this was a safe place—a place that could really help me.

I let my higher power take the lead and felt hope for the first time. For me, my suicide attempt was an act out of desperation and despair. My message of hope is that you can recover from both mental illness and addiction. My bipolar disorder has hurt both the quality of my life and recovery, so I must work on both—it is a matter of life or death. Today, I choose life.

Stage 1 of DBT

The first phase of DBT, Stage 1, focuses on gaining behavioral control. The shared goals of DBT and the Twelve Steps are to learn how to change your behaviors, emotions, and thoughts linked to addiction and to problems in accepting the reality that's causing misery and distress.

Here are some red flag thoughts and behaviors to watch out for:

- Not paying attention, feeling an empty hole inside, being out of touch with your sponsor, being judgmental, not attending AA/NA meetings, going to slippery places, that is, bars, the dealer's house, etc.
- Interpersonal conflict, stress, loneliness, isolation, not calling other AA/NA members, acting out
- Rollercoaster of extreme emotions, mood-dependent behavior, difficulties in regulating emotion, anger binges
- Impulsive behaviors, acting without thinking, difficulty accepting reality, willfulness, lying, deceitfulness.

Targets for Stage 1 of DBT

Dysfunctional state	Behavioral target
Destructive behavior	Gaining behavioral control
Interpersonal conflict	Defining boundaries and learning assertive behaviors
Refusing to admit powerlessness	Learning to surrender and trust the process
Abstinence-interfering behaviors	Commitment to abstinence

ACTIVITY: THE ALCOHOLIC/ADDICT PSYCHE VS. DRY DRUNK SYNDROME

"Dry drunk syndrome" was originally coined by one of the creators of the Twelve-Step program. It refers to a person's continuation of the same habits—actions and attitudes—they engaged in when they were using alcohol. Dry drunk syndrome sets the stage for a relapse. It is a risky place to stay.

In DBT, the addict mind is your state of mind when you have given in to addiction.[13] When you combine this DBT concept with Step One of AA/NA, we create the concept of the "alcoholic/addict psyche."

After referring to the examples, add your own experiences.

The alcoholic/addict psyche	Dry drunk syndrome
No one will know if I drink on the plane	I think it'll be okay if I drink on the plane
Telling my wife I'm going to work, but instead, I went to the bar to drink	Telling my wife I'm going to work, but I end up driving around the block where the bar is, but I don't go in
Romanticizing addiction	I no longer have an addiction problem
Not going to meetings	Cutting way back on meetings
I can drink once a week	I no longer have an alcohol problem

To reach the point where we can open ourselves to making necessary changes, we need to approach this possibility from a place of understanding and compassion. Embracing yourself as you are is the first step.

Radical Acceptance

Radical Acceptance means to stop fighting reality, responding with impulsive or destructive behaviors when things don't go your way, and letting go of the bitterness that is keeping you trapped in a cycle of suffering.[14]

Remember, you can't hate yourself into changing. Renowned psychologist Carl Rogers once said, "The curious paradox is that when I accept myself just as I am, then I can change."[15]

⬇ **ACTIVITY:** RADICAL ACCEPTANCE SKILLS

Practice meditation and relaxation techniques like breathing deeply, scanning your body and noticing where you feel tight, repeating a mantra, walking while meditating, practicing mindfulness, engaging in prayer, or reading and reflecting.

- Forgive yourself by admitting you made a mistake.
- Acknowledge reality by practicing honesty.
- Accept your humanity and imperfections as they are the touchstones for growth.
- Say to yourself, "I have no power over the past, the truth, and you."

Pick *two* Radical Acceptance skills.

Skill 1: Describe a situation you had trouble accepting and what skill(s) you used to cope with the reality of the problem.

. . . .

. . . .

. . . .

How effective was this skill in helping you cope with the above situation?

Not helpful | Somewhat helpful | Helpful | Very helpful | Extremely helpful

Skill 2: Describe a situation you had trouble accepting and what skill(s) you used to cope with the reality of the problem.

. . . .

. . . .

. . . .

How effective was this skill in helping you cope with the above situation?

Not helpful | Somewhat helpful | Helpful | Very helpful | Extremely helpful

The sober self

Now, to anchor ourselves in our reasons for committing to a life worth living, it's essential to note the differences between our sober self and our not-sober self.

Sobriety is a day at a time. Your sober self stays away from drinking or taking drugs and builds motivation to lead a meaningful life. Admitting and accepting your vulnerability is part of your sober self, as is abstaining from using alcohol or drugs. Your sober self learns through trial and error, and although you may fall, you don't stay down; you get up again and make the changes you need to get back on the beam.

To understand the difference between dry drunk syndrome and the sober self better, see the examples in the next activity.

ACTIVITY: DRY DRUNK SYNDROME VS. THE SOBER SELF

After referring to the examples, add your own.

Dry drunk syndrome	The sober self
I can do it alone	I don't have to recover alone; I have a community of support
I can quit anytime I want to	I'm deluding myself if I think I can drink safely
Stopping attendance of AA/NA meetings	The time I need to go to a meeting the most is when I don't think I need to go
I'm cured	I'm in recovery one day at a time
Hanging out in slippery places	Staying in the middle of the boat, with sober folks around me
Hungry, Angry, Lonely, Tired (HALT)	I'll check with myself to make sure I'm not hungry, angry, lonely, or tired, and, therefore, more vulnerable to a relapse
Keeping a stash, "just in case"	Not shutting the door leaves me vulnerable to relapse
Never again	One day at a time
Recovery is a matter of willpower	I am powerless over alcohol and drugs

After learning to identify and correct your stinking thinking and instead practice Radical Acceptance, abstinence becomes possible. In recognizing our powerlessness over drugs and alcohol, abstinence is crucial. Without it, sobriety becomes an unreachable goal.

⬇ ACTIVITY: CREATE AN ACTION PLAN TO STAY ABSTINENT TODAY

- Find a deeper conscience and meditate (e.g., practice mindfulness, read spiritual literature)
- Rely on a higher power (e.g., let go of being "right," pray, take a walk in nature)
- Participate in AA/NA meetings
- Write down a list of *five* (or more) things you are grateful for today
- Help someone today (e.g., ask a friend if there's anything you could help with)
- Get a sponsor if you don't have one, and work the Steps with that person.

What is your action plan to stay abstinent today?

. . . .

. . . .

What kind of meditation did you practice today?

. . . .

. . . .

How did you rely on a higher power today?

. . . .

. . . .

How did you participate in an AA/NA meeting? (For example did you share in a meeting today? Did you secretary a meeting?)

. . . .

. . . .

List *five* things you are grateful for today.

. . . .

. . . .

. . . .

. . . .

. . . .

Community reinforcement strategies combining DBT and the Twelve Steps

In AA/NA, the community reinforcement strategies found in the Twelve-Step program help to replace *addiction reinforcers* with *abstinence reinforcers*.

AA/NA meetings have helped millions of people all over the world. AA and NA are almost always the first recovery programs people think of.

Here are some ways to gain community reinforcement in AA/NA:

- Speak at an AA/NA meeting.
- Tell someone if you feel like drinking or picking up a drug.
- Find an AA/NA sponsor.
- Tell someone if you do drink or take drugs.

In DBT, community reinforcement means replacing addiction reinforcers with abstinence reinforcers. Share often at Twelve-Step meetings to get support from others. Go to fellowship (coffee, eating out) with other folks in AA/NA. Ask people in your support system, your sponsor, family, and friends, for help. Reinforcing abstinence is very important.

⊕ ACTIVITY: REINFORCING CLEAN AND SOBER BEHAVIORS

Who are the sober people you spend time with? Name *two*. Name *one* activity you've done together recently.

. . . .

. . . .

What clean and sober activities do you enjoy doing with other people? Name *two*. Describe what you did in each activity.

. . . .

. . . .

What steps have you taken to build a positive, clean, and sober community? Describe *two*.

. . . .

. . . .

How many days are you clean and sober today? Name *one* action step you have taken to meet this goal.

. . . .

. . . .

Healthy contrarianism

Even while remaining abstinent, many of us still have a desire to express our unbounded spirit, the side of ourselves that refuses to fit in a box. Without using alcohol or drugs, it's important to find new, healthy ways to be our true self.

Healthy contrarianism is a skill to practice new expressions of alcoholic or addict rebellious behavior that does not harm yourself or others. It's a valuable skill to add to your toolbox to help avoid the slippery slope of acting out. When I was younger, my father had a nickname for me, "Au Contraire," as I would lean into a backbend whenever he would ask me to do something.

Some examples of healthy contrarianism include:

- Join a protest or a cause you believe in.
- Wear your PJs all day.
- Wear all one color/all bright colors for a day.
- Dress up as your favorite character.
- Dye your hair an outrageous color.
- Walk backward around a running track.
- Write with your non-dominant hand for one day.
- Do something kind for a stranger.

ACTIVITY: DEVELOPING A PLAN FOR HEALTHY CONTRARIANISM

List a couple of healthy contrarianism actions you'd like to try:

1. . . . .

2. . . . .

Action 1: Describe the healthy contrarianism action you took instead of relapsing.

. . . .

. . . .

. . . .

. . . .

How effective was this action in helping you not relapse?

Not helpful | Somewhat helpful | Helpful | Very helpful | Extremely helpful

Action 2: Describe the healthy contrarianism action you took instead of relapsing.

. . . .

. . . .

. . . .

. . . .

How effective was this action in helping you not relapse?

Not helpful | Somewhat helpful | Helpful | Very helpful | Extremely helpful

Putting it all together

AA/NA focuses on the alcoholic or addict to acquire abstinence. People in early sobriety struggle with life-threatening behaviors (such as substance abuse or excessive drinking) and recovery-interfering behaviors (for example, stop attending meetings, being expelled from school, divorce). In working Step One, people in recovery move from admittance to acceptance by learning to surrender and trust the process. The Twelve Steps are not chronological—many people in recovery go back to a previous step if they get stuck on the Step they're currently working on.

In this chapter we learned about Stage 1 of DBT, which focuses on gaining behavioral control and accepting reality.

We learned the effectiveness of the DBT skill of Radical Acceptance: because fighting reality causes suffering. The DBT and AA/NA skills of community reinforcement include speaking at an AA/NA meeting, attending a meeting online, or going out to fellowship afterward.

We discussed how dry drunk syndrome sets the stage for a relapse. The sober self is a balanced self, open to both sides, committed to abstinence while considering the romantic notion of using. The addict mind in DBT is your state of mind when you have given into addiction. When you combine this DBT concept with Step One of AA/NA, we create the concept "alcohol/addict psyche."

We also reviewed the concept of healthy contrarianism; for example, practicing new skills of rebellious behavior that don't harm yourself or others.

As you gain confidence in adding DBT skills to AA/NA concepts, you have begun to lay the foundation of your recovery. The next chapter will build on the skills you've learned so far and work on integrating DBT skills into Step Two of AA/NA.

Chapter 2

Step Two: Hope

In this chapter:
- Activity: Working Step Two
- Activity: Understanding a higher power
→ What is willingness
  - Activity: Advantages and disadvantages of willingness vs. willfulness
  - Activity: Combating willfulness
→ Reasonable Mind
→ Emotion Mind
→ Wise Mind

Step Two	The DBT translation
Step Two is about willingness to find balance	DBT presents us with the dialectic of willingness or willfulness. Willingness is our ability to go with the flow; willfulness is our refusal to go with the flow

Step Two has to do with learning to make sound decisions. The "soundness of mind" discussed in Step Two of the "12 and 12" (Twelve Steps and Twelve Traditions) instead has to do with learning to make sound decisions. Step Two always makes me feel right at home at a meeting. I am grateful for this program, which has taught me to live life differently.

We learned that our drinking and drugging caused our life's craziness. Step Two asks us to believe in a higher power, which may be challenging. Choose a higher power that works for you. Instead of trying to understand what Step Two is on your own, ask other folks in the rooms of AA/NA, and attend Step study meetings.

Sanity is another word for balance. That's what we're reaching for in recovery, the hope that we will be restored to sanity. That's an important distinction because, as much as we hate to admit it, many of us don't want to give up the drama and chaos of our former life. It was exciting, but it had negative consequences. As DBT states, we're looking for the middle path, a balance. In Step Two, we're looking to a higher power to restore us to a balanced way of life.

Now we'll go into more depth and discuss the term "higher power." A higher power is any external factor that motivates and encourages you to stay sober.[16] This power transcends an individual's limitations and makes this belief accessible to all people, whether you are religious or not. Non-religious members have identified "God" as an acronym for "Good Orderly Direction." Others even refer to it as "Group of Drunks/Druggies" or "the Great Out-Doors." What's essential is choosing something greater than yourself to help you achieve balance. You have the choice to decide what a higher power means to you.

Belief fits into the sphere of mindfulness and DBT as smoothly as the final piece to a jigsaw puzzle. A belief in spirituality, God, or religion can be a tremendous support for many of us. In addition, incorporating mindfulness into our lives clarifies our perception of "the here, the now." We sometimes forget to be mindful of the present.

Mindfulness gives us gratitude for the many blessings in our lives. There is much that can't be explained by science, potentially being proof of faith. Faith and God also fit into mindfulness because it presents understanding the events around us, from the most significant event down to the minutest. Step Two sets the stage of hope and shows us a way forward

ACTIVITY: WORKING STEP TWO

As part of the recovery process, it's beneficial to ask ourselves questions about Step Two.

Give *two* examples of decisions you made (during your alcoholism or addiction) that were not in your best interests.

. . . .

. . . .

. . . .

Have you faced any challenges in accepting that there is a power greater than yourself?

. . . .

. . . .

. . . .

In a couple of sentences, describe how you came to believe in a higher power.

. . . .

. . . .

. . . .

List *two* examples of a higher power working in your life.

. . . .

. . . .

. . . .

ACTIVITY: UNDERSTANDING A HIGHER POWER

Define what "GOD" means to you (e.g., **G**roup **O**f **D**runks, **G**reat **O**ut**D**oors, **G**ood **O**rderly **D**irection).

. . . .

. . . .

. . . .

What is your current concept of a higher power?

. . . .

. . . .

. . . .

What role does spirituality play in your life today?

. . . .

. . . .

. . . .

Were you ever angry at your higher power? Describe a situation that triggered that anger.

. . . .

. . . .

. . . .

What is willingness

The concept of willingness is essential to recovery.

Willingness, simply put, is the act of doing the next right thing in any situation. To do that, you assess effectiveness (the last skill of mindfulness). The skill of being effective in the context of DBT involves "doing what works, doing what moves you closer to your long-term goals, and doing what you need to do to get your needs met. So the first step to effectiveness is to figure out what your goal is: what it is that you're trying to accomplish."[17]

Willingness is listening attentively and following your Wise Mind. A Wise Mind can see the value in both reason and emotion and choose the middle path. We are aware of all our senses in the present and our physical responses to them.

Willingness opens the doors to our spiritual connection to the universe while grounding us in our immediate surroundings. Do not, however, mistake willingness for denial or oversimplification of our struggles. It is, instead, a pathway to connecting to everyone around you.

The DBT model of willingness is similar to AA/NA's approach to willingness. AA/NA have several acronyms, slogans, and sayings that support the program's message while helping you remember skills on your recovery journey, in this case the *HOW principle* (*Honesty, Open-mindedness, and Willingness*). (Although note that the HOW principle of AA/NA is different from the HOW skill of DBT.)

HOW PRINCIPLE
Recovery programs tell us that there are three things we need to recover from alcoholism or addiction:

- *Honesty:* Mindfulness starts with inner reflection; likewise, recovery begins with honesty. Unless you are honest with yourself and others in your life, you cannot begin the process of healing. If we're not honest with ourselves, we cannot get better. At the same time, we need support to get better, but lying to our therapists, families, or any help can interfere with our recovery. Lying can be unconscious or conscious.
- *Open-mindedness:* After practicing honesty, the next step is to work on being open, and being open-minded means accepting the opportunities to get better and understanding what is beneficial to us, even if the approach sounds wrong, crazy, complicated, or stupid. It means that we listen to others and that we refrain from making any judgments.
- *Willingness:* The third element for recovery in this principle is willingness. Building on the previous two pieces, when you are open-minded, you are ready to listen and take a step forward in practicing hard skills.

What is willfulness?
In DBT, willingness refers to recognizing the reality of the situation and being an effective problem-solver. Willfulness is a little like a child's temper tantrum. Everyone has experienced willfulness at some point in their recovery. It is fighting what is happening and refusing to tolerate the facts around you. For example, you receive an eviction notice. Initially, you tell yourself you need to deal with it. However, you change your mind, and acting willfully, you put the eviction notice away.

In DBT, willfulness is an act of stubbornness and is a deliberate lack of discipline. Being willful is the complete opposite of the concept of willingness. When you are willful, you are saying "no" to life, reality, and the truth. Running away from a situation or a problem only makes matters worse. Willfulness means trying to fix everything that is not in your control. Sitting in discomfort sometimes is okay.

Unfair situations arise all the time, and they are part of life. When feeling hopeless and miserable, giving up is often the easy way out. However, not doing anything about a situation and complacency is also being willful and ineffective. When you are constantly making excuses, that is willfulness, not recovery. In other words, "I want what I want when I want it."

ACTIVITY: ADVANTAGES AND DISADVANTAGES OF WILLINGNESS VS. WILLFULNESS

Name a situation where you *willingly* accepted it as it is. Write down the advantages and disadvantages you faced by doing so.

. . . .

. . . .

. . . .

Advantages	Disadvantages

Name a situation where you *willfully* rejected it as it is. Write down the advantages and disadvantages you faced by doing so.

. . . .

. . . .

. . . .

Advantages	Disadvantages

ACTIVITY: COMBATING WILLFULNESS

Describe a situation in which you acted willfully.

· ·

· ·

Reflect on the situation and radically accept what was happening at that moment. How did radically accepting your willfulness help you to move forward?

· ·

· ·

· ·

Try a willing posture by relaxing your shoulders and opening your arms. Did that relieve any tension you've been storing in your body?

· ·

· ·

· ·

The serenity prayer is familiar to most folks in recovery: "God grant me the serenity to accept the things I cannot change; courage to change the things I can; and wisdom to know the difference."

The goals of DBT are behavioral control, emotional expression, accountability, and achieving transcendence. You can accomplish these goals by building courage, serenity, and the wisdom to only change what is within your control. You can achieve these goals by practicing core mindfulness and distress tolerance skills to accept your reality.

Life's challenges fit into two broad categories: issues with emotions and difficulties with thinking. Emotional problems have to do with acting out the way you feel (impulsivity), moodiness, anger, anxiety, and confused feelings. Any combination of such issues can lead to interpersonal chaos, confusion about self, or the inability to regulate your mind; in other words, misery and distress.

To counter this, one of the goals of DBT is achieving a balanced state of mind, a Wise Mind. As you learn and practice more skills throughout the book, you will develop a Wise Mind sense. Changing your behaviors, managing your emotions, and becoming conscious of your life patterns benefit from using your Wise Mind. To understand Wise Mind, you need to understand two states of mind: Reasonable Mind and Emotion Mind.[18]

Reasonable Mind

A Reasonable Mind is entirely rational, with no room for emotions. In this state, you solely base your judgments on what makes sense—evidence, facts—and are generally detached. You often use your past to gauge your responses to current circumstances. This state of Reasonable Mind is essential to learning skills.

Some examples of a Reasonable Mind include making a budget and sticking to it, baking a cake from a recipe, or figuring out a bus route. The Reasonable Mind looks at the facts of a situation and is very logical. The Reasonable Mind is void of emotion. Instead, it looks at the attributes of a problem. An excellent example of someone in Reasonable Mind is Mr Spock in the *Star Trek* television and film series. Spock loved to offer his logical perspective on life to the volatile Captain Kirk, commenting on society and humanity, offering an insight into the Vulcan mind. When faced with emotional responses from Captain Kirk, Spock would often say, "That is highly illogical."

Emotion Mind

Emotion Mind is the state where your emotions are driving the bus. In Emotion Mind, you tend to react in a fast, unfiltered manner rather than respond. It is the opposite of Reasonable Mind, which is devoid of any emotional weight.

Going on a trip on impulse without making plans ahead of time, buying something expensive that you can't afford, or moving across the country to be with someone you just met on Facebook—these are examples of acting out of Emotion Mind. Other examples include sending an email, text, or making a phone call as a reaction to what someone said without thinking it through.

Wise Mind

In Buddhism, Wise Mind refers to an ideal state of mind with a practiced sense of intuition and flexible, adaptive, and holistic thinking. In DBT, the "middle path" integrates Emotion Mind and Reasonable Mind. Thus, the DBT Wise Mind overlaps two extreme ends on the spectrum—Emotion Mind on the left and Reasonable Mind on the right. You are either overly emotional or overly rational in your decisions and behaviors if you are on either side of the spectrum. In Wise Mind, you can integrate facts and logic from Reasonable Mind and connect to others with compassion by using Emotion Mind. In Wise Mind, you focus on a functional and practical approach to conflict resolution.

The core sense of Wise Mind involves a deep understanding of intuitive knowing. In this sense, intuition goes beyond reason.[19] This deep-seated intuition comes from an integration of "direct experience, immediate cognition, and the grasping of the meaning, significance, or truth of an event without relying on intellectual analysis."[20]

It might seem like an overwhelming or intimidating concept to master, or a state that is impossible to reach, but I can assure you we all have a Wise Mind. Like any skill, easily accessing Wise Mind is something you can achieve with repeated practice. Applying the concept of Wise Mind to real-life scenarios can help you observe when, where, and how you are using it.

Some examples of Wise Mind include making a graceful exit during an argument with a loved one, taking time to meditate in the morning or during a busy workday to get centered, or going for a walk when feeling stuck or frustrated.

Putting it all together

After admitting you have a problem with drinking and drugging in Step One, we moved on to Step Two—finding a higher power, and, in the process, balance, and believing that a higher power can restore you to sanity.

We work Step Two by becoming more willing and less willful. Being willful hinders us from believing in a power greater than ourselves. We can combat willfulness by understanding the three states of mind—Reasonable, Emotion, and Wise Mind.

Reasonable Mind is the logical state of mind you use when your goal is to accomplish a concrete task that requires evidence. Emotion Mind is the state of mind that uses emotions and feelings rather than logic. Wise Mind is the utopic middle ground where you are aware of both your feelings and emotions from Emotion Mind and the facts and logic from Reasonable Mind, and act accordingly. Understanding the concept of Wise Mind is beneficial for radically accepting your situation and finding a higher power. Now we're ready for Step Three—surrendering your will and your life to a power greater than yours.

Chapter 3

Step Three: Surrender

In this chapter:
→ Turning the mind
  – Activity: A higher power of your understanding
→ Wise Mind
→ Values and priorities
  – Activity: Defining your core values
  – Activity: Identifying your values
  – Activity: Values discussion questions
→ Letting go of emotional suffering

Step Three	The DBT translation
Step Three is seeking knowledge of a higher power's will for you and deciding to turn over your will and be restored to balance	We surrender our old way and trust DBT skills to teach us a new way of life

Turning my will and my life over to my higher power in Step Three gave me the strength and hope to face life with God's care. I wanted to be sober very badly, so I tried everything people suggested in meetings. It took quite a while, but eventually, I chose to turn my will and my life over to the care of God as I understand God.

Turning over your will as outlined in this Step is critical if you are to progress in your healing and growth in recovery. To truly "let go and let God," you need to give up control.

The following acronym, MAPS, will help guide you and make the process straightforward:

- *Learn to Meditate:* Meditation provides a tremendous benefit because it can quiet the mind by focusing on the body in the present moment. In early recovery, we are restless, and the mind will be filled with past events or worries about what the future may bring. By focusing on what you can, you are willing to accept the guidance of others and your higher power.
- *Ask for help:* Asking for help is a crucial step in learning to turn your will over to a higher power. You asked for help by attending your first AA/NA meeting. Remember, you don't have to make this journey alone. If you have questions or are feeling insecure or unsure, ask for help!
- *Practice acceptance:* One stumbling block I have encountered in recovery is demanding that the world be how I want it. I used to believe true happiness was what I wanted from the world instead of accepting that the world is what it is. As a result, I had to learn ways to exist in that world. At first, this wasn't easy, and it still isn't!

  I am taking life on life's terms and understanding that the only thing I can control is my response to it and focusing on what I need to do. Fix it? Change it? Accept it? Practicing acceptance does not mean we have to be resigned to what life hands us. It means waking up each morning and saying "This is what I have been given today—what do I plan to do about it?" and then do the next right thing. Acceptance is the core. Acceptance is: whether I like it or not, this is the reality of the moment. So, the next step is, given that reality, how can we respond with joy and ease?
- *Serenity prayer:* To get the benefits from prayer, you don't necessarily have to believe it will help—just act as if it will. Just as there are many different people, no matter where you pray, how you pray, or whom you pray to, it is vital that you fully engage in the practice of prayer. My favorite version of the serenity prayer is by Father Tom Weston, a Jesuit priest.

God grant me the Serenity to accept the things I cannot change.
The Past, the Truth, and You!
The courage to change the things I can
Me, Myself, and I; my thought, my attitudes, my behavior
And the wisdom to know the difference.

Turning the mind

Just as turning over your life and will is critical if you progress in your healing and growth in recovery, "turning the mind" is an essential concept to serenity.

In DBT, the practical skill used in accepting the situation in these circumstances is turning the mind. You turn the mind towards acceptance, a path that alleviates your suffering. At the same time, you turn the mind away from negative thoughts you are holding about the situation.

The first action is to identify and observe that you are not accepting the situation, and only then can you commit to practicing acceptance. At first it might seem like an easy way to deny, ignore, avoid, or resist reality when confronted with a challenging, stressful, or overwhelming situation. Looking at reality can be tough. However, the only way to deal with it is to acknowledge it.

Without consistent personal affirmation and a commitment to acceptance, emotions like anger and bitterness can make your life miserable. You can always walk away from the path of pain towards a better life by remembering to turn your mind.

The three simple steps to turn your mind are:

1. Observe your resistance.
2. Commit to accepting your reality:
   a. Commit to acceptance, over and over again.
   b. Make a plan for when you fall out of acceptance.
3. Ask yourself: have I turned the pain, fear, grief, or anger over?

Acknowledging reality is the first essential action of Step Three. The reality is that we all need help, and there is no shame in asking and getting it. Turning the mind is similar to the concept of turning your will and life over to the care of a higher power. Through turning the mind, we open ourselves to experiencing relief from distress. By turning over our will, we also let go of distress by allowing a power greater than ourselves to care for us.

Our logical mind believes that surrendering our will and life to a higher power equals being insignificant and powerless. Becoming willing is itself an act of will on our part. Self-will is to be selfish, self-centered, and too proud to accept help. When my emotions are off or I find myself battling overwhelming urges to drink, run, or escape, I get quiet with myself and do a mental scan of the first three Steps. Have I turned my will and my life over to my higher power?

⊛ ACTIVITY: A HIGHER POWER OF YOUR UNDERSTANDING

Consider how acting on your own free will has impacted your life. Write down *two* instances below.

. . . .

. . . .

. . . .

How did acting on your self-will affect others? Give *two* examples.

. . . .

. . . .

. . . .

Write down *two* action steps you are willing to start to change the above.

. . . .

. . . .

. . . .

How do you define your higher power?

. . . .

. . . .

. . . .

In Step Two, we began to cover the concept of Wise Mind. We can now continue to explore the application of Wise Mind in further detail.

Wise Mind

Wise Mind is the unique integration of Emotion Mind and Reasonable Mind, where you are centered and in control of your emotions and logic. In addition, this state can be personal in the sense of having a center of awareness in your mind and body, for example your intuition, sixth sense, or a gut feeling.

There are a few ways to practice Wise Mind:[21]

- Learn to focus on a single task or issue. You may find it helpful to set a timer for 10, 20, or 30 minutes to break up a task into smaller chunks.
- Start practicing breathing in and out deeply. While you breathe in, think of a question and pay attention to your thoughts that emerge when you exhale slowly.

A great way to remember these skills is by using the acronym PAGES. Try a different letter each time.

- *Put away:*
    - Put your pain in a God box—find a special box that can serve as a place to store worries and things outside your control. (Tip: use sticky notes.)
    - Take your dog for a walk.
    - Take a time out from the problem.
- *Act:*
    - Engage in a physical activity you enjoy.
    - Listen to some music.
    - Plan a day out with a loved one.
- *Give:*
    - Donate things you don't need.
    - Reach out to a loved one just to say "hi."
    - Do one meaningful thing for someone else.
- *Emotions:*
    - Watch a scary or a funny movie.
    - Read correspondences between you and a loved one.
    - Put on an outfit that brings you joy.
- *Sensations:*
    - Hum a song.
    - Observe the nature outside your window.
    - Hold an ice pack.
    - Brush your hair.

The goal of DBT is to achieve or reach a state of Wise Mind. Not just the intersection of Emotion Mind and Reasonable Mind, Wise Mind is characterized by a deep sense of understanding and intuition. When you realize this, the concept of Radical Acceptance hits home. When we begin to experience life's ups and downs with acceptance, we can start to live without push or pull. You can respond to risk-taking with deep compassion instead of reactivity.

Moving forward, we are now going to look in detail at your values and priorities. What's important to you? How did you come to that decision?

Values and priorities

Why do we need to evaluate our values and priorities, and what role do they play in making positive changes in our lives? Understanding our values and priorities in DBT is an interpersonal skill.

Connecting with your true priorities means understanding what is important to you and what you want. These priorities do not include expectations of you from other people. The goal is to strive for a balance that allows you to live your life successfully. So how does this apply to your life? Your values are the things that you hold sacred in your daily life and work. They are also the indicators you use to determine whether your life is on the right path.

When your actions and behaviors reflect your values, you are satisfied with life, and you are content. On the other hand, when your actions and behaviors don't reflect your values, you feel dissatisfied. That's why it's important to identify and define your values.

Accepting your values and living in a way that honors them makes life much easier. You could start by asking yourself specific questions about your life to make better decisions for yourself:

- Should I compromise or be firm with my decision to stay clean and sober?
- Should I do some more "research," or should I talk to my sponsor when I have an urge?

Take the time to understand your true priorities in life. How do you define these values? A great place to start is by reflecting on your past and recognizing the times you felt confident and content in your choices, and if that made you feel good.

⊕ ACTIVITY: DEFINING YOUR CORE VALUES

Love	Resilience	Simplicity
Reliability	Attractiveness	Calmness
Abundance	Ethics	Family
Daring	Making a difference	Performance
Intuition	Resourcefulness	Stability
Acceptance	Autonomy	Caring
Decisiveness	Excellence	Friendships
Joy	Teamwork	Success
Achievement	Self-control	Challenge
Dedication	Boldness	Proactivity
Kindness	Originality	Compassion
Professionalism	Selflessness	Flexibility
Empathy	Brilliance	Security
Learning	Ambition	Uniqueness
Relationships	Encouragement	Happiness

Inspired by the list above, list *three* core values.

For each core value, write an example of how/why it resonates with you.

Core value 1:

. . . .

. . . .

Core value 2:

. . . .

. . . .

Core value 3:

. . . .

. . . .

ACTIVITY: IDENTIFYING YOUR VALUES

Name a person you respect or admire. What do you think they value?

. . . .

. . . .

What values do you share with them?

. . . .

. . . .

What values do you hold that are different?

. . . .

. . . .

List your top three values:

. . . .

. . . .

. . . .

What is your top value, and why?

. . . .

. . . .

While values are the fundamental beliefs that help guide you through your life, priorities are decisions or rules that govern your behavior and attitudes. Unfortunately, these can be so ingrained in us that sometimes we only notice them when we come up against them.

What impact do you want to have on the lives around you, and how do you want people to remember you? What are you prioritizing at the moment, and what are you prioritizing for the future? These priorities help you make choices. You decide how to make each day count and take it one day at a time.

When I became a new mom, I was busy from 6am to midnight every day. I had a 40-hour per week job, a private practice, a partner, a sponsor, friends, etc. But I hardly had any time to be with my daughter, partner, friends, or myself. I needed to look at my priorities. I was exhausted. My life did not reflect my value of spending quality time with my family and friends. I needed to make changes to reflect my priorities. I gradually let go of my private practice. My partner and I scheduled a date night every week. I made time for one or two friends and asked other friends to stay in touch over the phone, text, or video chat. I took the first step towards a life that reflected my values.

ACTIVITY: VALUES DISCUSSION QUESTIONS

Values tend to change as we pass through different stages of our lives. Let's reflect on your life when you were using or drinking, versus now, when you are clean and sober. How do your values differ, and what are their similarities?

Your values in the past	Your values now

While you have made positive changes to your behaviors and reevaluated your values, what are some values you hope to attain? Compare your current list and what you aim to accomplish.

The values you want to achieve

When you incorporate your values into priorities, you can now approach decisions with confidence and clarity. When you do that, you also consider what's most beneficial for your current and future happiness. This process is not easy, but it makes it simpler to make the right decisions that are true to you in the long run.

Letting go of emotional suffering

In this section, we will go over methods to help us let go of emotional distress. It is an extremely challenging step to practice letting go of painful and negative emotions.

Getting rid of the emotional distress brought on by your emotions is not the same as getting rid of the feelings themselves. You don't have to push away your feelings or ignore them. You can, instead, discover how to accept the validity of your feelings.

Six steps to mindfully deal with difficult emotions

1. *Turn toward your emotions with acceptance.* Be aware of the emotion and where it is in your body.
2. *Identify and label the emotion.* To stay mindful, say to yourself, "This is anger" or "This is anxiety."
3. *Accept your emotions.* Don't deny the emotion. Acknowledge and accept that it is there.
4. *Realize the impermanence of your emotions.* Even if the emotion feels overwhelming, remember, "This too shall pass."
5. *Inquire and investigate.* Ask yourself, "What triggered me? Why do I feel this way?"
6. *Let go of the need to control your emotions.* Be open to the outcome of your emotions and what unfolds.

Putting it all together

In this chapter, we recognize Step Three is a decision we make daily. No matter how many times we take our will back, in the next moment, we can do the next right thing.

We looked at DBT skills that can assist us in turning things over. Turning the mind helps us move through difficult emotions without avoiding them. Meditation provides a tremendous benefit because it can quiet the mind by focusing on the body in the present moment. Asking for help is a crucial step in learning to turn your will over to a higher power. By taking life on life's terms, we understand that the only thing we can control is our response to it.

Wise Mind is the unique integration of Emotion Mind and Reasonable Mind, where you are centered and in control of your emotions and logic. In this state, you can utilize both states of mind to make difficult decisions unique to you.

We learned DBT distraction skills, such as going for a walk or reaching out to a loved one. Understanding your priorities means recognizing what is important to you and what you want. Your values are the things that you hold sacred in your daily life and work.

Finally, we reviewed ways you can let go of emotional suffering, including accepting, labeling, and realizing the impermanence of your emotions. Inquire and investigate what triggered you, so you can move on to the next step.

Chapter 4

Step Four: Finding Courage

In this chapter:
- Activity: Step Four inventory
- Activity: Step Four
→ FAST skill: Self-respect effectiveness
→ What are thought distortions?
- Activity: Combating thought distortions
→ Myths about your emotions
- Activity: Myths about your emotions
→ RAIN, a mindfulness tool
- Activity: RAIN

Step Four	The DBT translation
Step Four is about becoming willing to move forward in recovery by honestly examining your past substance use and actions, and how it has affected you and others	The DBT skill of actions based on values asks us to think about what exactly we would do to live our lives according to the values we choose. This involves looking at specific actions we engage in

My first Step Four felt like a memoir. I wrote pages and pages, forgetting at times that it was more important to be "rigorously honest." Sharing my Step Four with my sponsor was very healing. Many a Step Four has been a guiding force in my sobriety journey and discovering who I am. Getting outside help, learning DBT skills, and attending therapy regularly have enabled me to fill the gaps that AA/NA couldn't.

Are you ready to give up who you are to be who you can be? Some old-timers in AA/NA use the column approach in the *Big Book*, which looks at our resentments, fears, and sexual conduct. So, feel the fear and do it anyway.

Start writing stuff down, focusing on past events in your life, including your weaknesses and strengths.

Sometimes, if a sponsee is feeling down on themselves, I'll ask them to add the columns "What's good about me?" and "What are my strengths?" I also ask, "What do you get out of this defect of character?" There is usually a payoff in our behavior, even if it's negative.

My sponsor set a date to hear my Step Five, which helped me not to procrastinate. The hardest part was seeing my dishonest behaviors together on a piece of paper. When I finished, my sponsor expressed compassion as I revealed my worst secrets. The benefits of completing Step Four are solid sobriety, spiritual growth, and mending your relationships with your higher power, yourself, and other human beings. We're only as sick as our secrets. While working on my Step Four inventory, I got a new perspective on the bigger picture of my patterns in most situations.

By now, you've realized that recovery is a process, not an event. So, before we can keep moving forward in our recovery, we need a framework to sort out fact from fiction. The Step Four inventory is that framework.

Step Four of AA/NA helps you identify negative thoughts, emotions, and actions that have become part of your character. Before entering recovery, we justified, rationalized, and projected our problems onto other people, places, and things. Finally, you are taking responsibility for your behavior, the good, bad, and the ugly. Some of it won't be pretty. But we need to write it down, as embarrassing as it may be. While writing out your inventory, you will get to examine all of your fears, pride, resentments/anger, self-will and self-pity, guilt/shame, relationships, sex/abuse, secrets, and assets.

Similarly, in AA/NA, Step Four is a method for learning about ourselves, finding our character assets, and identifying the exact nature of our wrongs. Thus, the inventory process is also an avenue to freedom. Most of us have felt isolated and different long before we drank and took drugs. Your inventory will open your eyes to the unresolved pain and conflicts in the past.

In Step Four you will discover that most of your troubles are of your own making. You will see how you played a role in how your conduct has harmed others. These are the very things that have blocked us from our higher power, the only power that can remove the alcoholic or addiction obsession.

Resentment is the "number one" offender. It destroys more alcoholics and addicts than anything else. All forms of spiritual disease stem from it, or we have been mentally and physically ill but have been spiritually sick.[22]

ACTIVITY: STEP FOUR INVENTORY

To better understand these resentments, use this activity to create what Bill W. calls a "grudge list." List your resentments and how they are affecting your life.

My resentments	Why I'm resentful	This affected my... (Circle those that apply)	Defects of character (Circle those that apply)	Blocks (Ways in which this resentment has blocked you from your higher power and others)	Payoff (Ways in which this resentment has benefitted you)
"I'm resentful at..."	"Because they..."	Self-esteem, finances, ambitions, relationships	Pride, anger, greed, gluttony, lust, envy, sloth, fear		
"I'm resentful at..."	"Because they..."	Self-esteem, finances, ambitions, relationships	Pride, anger, greed, gluttony, lust, envy, sloth, fear		
"I'm resentful at..."	"Because they..."	Self-esteem, finances, ambitions, relationships	Pride, anger, greed, gluttony, lust, envy, sloth, fear		
"I'm resentful at..."	"Because they..."	Self-esteem, finances, ambitions, relationships	Pride, anger, greed, gluttony, lust, envy, sloth, fear		
"I'm resentful at..."	"Because they..."	Self-esteem, finances, ambitions, relationships	Pride, anger, greed, gluttony, lust, envy, sloth, fear		
"I'm resentful at..."	"Because they..."	Self-esteem, finances, ambitions, relationships	Pride, anger, greed, gluttony, lust, envy, sloth, fear		

What is an overarching pattern you've noticed in your blocks?

. . . .

. . . .

What fears do you have about doing your inventory?

. . . .

. . . .

⊕ ACTIVITY: STEP FOUR

Step Four involves making a list of the people, places, and things that you have caused harm. Now that you've completed the list, analyze your fears to see how each item affected your life and decisions. Then look at the role you played in each situation that inflicted harm or caused resentment.

What behaviors make you feel better about yourself? List *two*.

. . . .

. . . .

What behaviors make you feel worse about yourself? List *two*.

. . . .

. . . .

List *two* behaviors that help you build relationships with others.

. . . .

. . . .

List *two* behaviors that have harmed your relationships with others.

. . . .

. . . .

List *two* qualities people say they like about you, and *two* qualities they don't.

. . . .

. . . .

FAST skill: Self-respect effectiveness

Sometimes we find ourselves betraying our values and beliefs for the sake of a relationship. The DBT acronym for self-respect effectiveness is FAST (Fair, Apologies, Stick, Truthful).[23] The interpersonal skill of FAST can increase the likelihood of positive outcomes. When used effectively, FAST skills help you convey your needs and wishes clearly, without the other person having to read your mind. It allows you to ask for what you want respectfully while considering the other person's needs and wants.

Being effective means behaving in a way that honors both you and your relationships with others. It's essential in any interpersonal situation to be mindful of your actions during and after the interaction. Now, let's look at this acronym in more depth:

- *Fair:* Be fair to yourself and the other person. Both are important. In any relationship, it's essential to consider both the other person's needs and your own. Be assertive, use your voice, speak your truth. Listen to the other person, reflect on what you heard them say, and then give your response to what they said. In turn, listen to their reflection of what you said and their response. Then, be open to a discussion or possible resolution.
- *(No) Apologies:* Early in recovery, I apologized for everything—for example, when someone stepped on my toe, I apologized! When I started my internship as a social worker in Brooklyn, New York, I even apologized for not knowing specific policies and procedures. I remember my supervisor saying, "How could you know? You just started to work here!"

  Using this skill, I gained awareness when I apologized for making a request, apologized for breathing, taking up space, or just being alive! I'm learning I don't need to apologize for having my own opinion or disagreeing with others.

  Many people in recovery struggle with over-apologizing, which perpetuates low self-esteem, feelings of frustration, resentment, self-loathing, and self-betrayal. Over-apologizing is the opposite of self-respect. As you gain awareness, start asking yourself, "Wait, why am I apologizing?" Take a spot inventory. "Did I do or say something that warrants an apology, or am I over-apologizing?"

People often apologize to avoid conflict or have difficulty tolerating someone being angry with them. Becoming aware of this habit can help raise your self-respect.

- *Stick to values: To thine own self be true.* This phrase is on the back of every AA coin. In other words, trust your gut and don't go against what you know is right for you. For example, your friends want to go to a concert, but you have difficulty being around alcohol in your early sobriety. Also, you need to be at work at 8am the next day. This situation doesn't work for you. Use your voice and offer suggestions.
- *(Be) Truthful:* Tell the truth. The truth stands on its own. Don't fall into the trap of justifying your actions, embellishing, or making excuses. You might often find you're trying to avoid conflict because you don't want to hurt the other person's feelings. Dishonesty is probably the single biggest obstacle to recovery.[24]

The FAST skill is an essential component of communication. It allows you to maintain your self-respect and requires you to be truthful about the problems (how you frame them) and not sacrifice your values or integrity. Telling only half the truth is still a lie. Lying is harmful to your relationships with others and yourself.

What are thought distortions?

Thought distortions are irrational thoughts that can influence emotions. It's not that your brain is trying to control you negatively; it's that after years of telling yourself certain assumptions, you start to believe these assumptions are valid. The key is, don't believe everything you think.

Thought distortions happen when we are stuck so fully in one point of view that our thoughts morph into a more "extreme" version of what we may really, truly, think. A common type of thought distortion is making judgments of others and ourselves. For instance, I have a long-time friend I think the world of. But last year, she never got in touch, not even to wish me a happy birthday. I was heartbroken. We've been friends for more than a decade and she had never forgotten my birthday before. I thought, "She must not care about me anymore! Why else couldn't she at least send a quick text message? I won't wish her a happy birthday then, either." This is black and white thinking.

In this situation, the jump to an irrational conclusion—"she must not like me"—is an instance of distorted thinking. In this situation, I could, instead, rationalize my response. Stepping outside of the situation, I could point out that there are plenty of reasons she might not have known or remembered to reach out for my birthday. Maybe she is overwhelmed with work, or never had the date memorized, or something else is going on—maybe I could even check in on *her*. By ignoring further complexities of the situation, I allowed myself to give in to black and white thinking.

Black and white thinking is a tendency to see things in extremes when we are unable to reconcile the existence of a middle ground.[25] My friend is neither flawless nor terrible. Mistakes are made. Slip-ups happen. Sometimes friends do drift away—but sometimes they come back. No one is perfect. We are all human!

Black and white thinking also occurs in other situations we are reactive to, such as what we may perceive as an honest perception of our own faults or limits. While it can feel valid to be self-critical, awareness of faults and limitations can often be misleading. It's important that we don't give these thought processes the power to hold us back through their distortion. Instead, through learning to apply healthy thought responses, we will find that we can feel empowered in using a critical but forgiving eye to motivate ourselves onward.

Sometimes our brains learn to behave in ways that are in conflict with our true intentions and goals. The following activity provides the opportunity to address areas where thought distortions have a negative effect on our lives.

ACTIVITY: COMBATING THOUGHT DISTORTIONS

Practice writing down a healthy response to your thought distortions.

Problem 1: Black and white thinking.

Example of a negative thought: "I relapsed again; I'm a total failure. I can't do anything right." The cognitive distortion here is black and white thinking.

Healthier response: "Relapse is serious, but it doesn't mean I am a total failure."

Now fill in your own examples.

Negative thought:

. . . .

. . . .

Healthier response:

. . . .

. . . .

Problem 2: Projecting, which refers to unconsciously taking unwanted emotions or traits you dislike about yourself and attributing them to others.

Example of projecting a negative thought: "If I open my mouth, everyone will think I'm stupid, and they'll hate me." The cognitive distortion here is self-labeling.

Healthier response: "Why do I care so much what other people think of me? I am here to help myself; I earned my seat here."

Now fill in your own examples.

Negative thought:

. . . .

. . . .

Healthier response:

. . . .

. . . .

Problem 3: Overwhelming negative impulse.

Example of a negative thought: "I have to pick up a drink/drug when I get angry."

Healthier response: "I can deal with this. I am stronger than I think I am."

Now fill in your own examples.

Negative thought:

. . . .

. . . .

Healthier response:

. . . .

. . . .

Problem 4: Future-tripping, when we spend our time thinking in terms of the future, usually anticipating a negative outcome.

Example of a negative thought: "I know things aren't going to work out…I can feel it." The cognitive distortion here is fortune telling.

Healthier response: "Just because things feel bad doesn't mean they are bad."

Now fill in your own examples.

Negative thought:

. . . .

. . . .

Healthier response:

. . . .

. . . .

Myths about your emotions

As a society, we regard displaying emotions as a sign of weakness. While it is healthy to act professionally and to rationally express feelings, allowing yourself to be vulnerable is not a sign of weakness. On the contrary, it denotes strength and emotional intelligence. Let's take a look at a few common myths about your feelings and how to disprove them:

- *Myth 1: I have intense emotions, which must indicate that I am out of control.* Feeling intense emotions and responding to them are two different things. The latter focuses on your behavior, which you do have control over. Handling a range of emotions is a powerful way to support your emotional wellbeing and improve your ability to respond appropriately. You make your best decisions when you listen to your heart and mind—your thoughts and your emotions.
- *Myth 2: I need to suppress my feelings, or I will act out on them.* DBT teaches you skills to regulate your emotions. Communicating how you feel demonstrates your willingness to be vulnerable and a level of trust in that relationship. Learning to deal with uncomfortable feelings is an excellent step to creating the best life for yourself. You will realize that while they are uncomfortable, they are also tolerable. Suppressing and avoiding painful emotions only increases your suffering.
- *Myth 3: I need to feel a certain way because everyone else feels like that.* What others feel about a particular situation may not be what you think. It is typical for different people to have different emotional reactions. It is not helpful to pressure yourself to conform your views to theirs.
- *Myth 4: I am my emotions.* You are more than your emotions. If you base your identity on your feelings, you will feel disoriented and struggle to find a stable sense of self. While it is normal to experience multiple emotions at once, learning to monitor them keeps them from over-whelming you.
- *Myth 5: I feel these emotions; they must be true.* Feelings are not facts. But remember that your emotions are natural responses to your environment, and your values and beliefs frame them.
- *Myth 6: I can't be creative without intense emotions.* Emotions can contribute and support creativity, but it's a myth that you can't be creative without them. The more DBT skills you learn for healthily dealing with your emotions, the easier it will be to be productive and make better life decisions for yourself.

Intense emotions can be overpowering, but they are manageable. Keep in mind that you are resilient! You can't will them away, but you can learn to help relieve the discomfort that comes with them and the distress that comes from ignoring them. We'll go over this skill in the following activity to help you change your mindset, cultivate gratitude, and practice mindfulness so you can treat yourself with more empathy and care.

ACTIVITY: MYTHS ABOUT YOUR EMOTIONS

Part 1: Circle the number that denotes your level of belief in these myths about your emotions (1 being the least you identify with and 5 being the most you identify with).

I have intense emotions, which must indicate that I am out of control	1	2	3	4	5
I need to suppress my feelings, or I will act out on them	1	2	3	4	5
I need to feel a certain way because everyone else feels like that	1	2	3	4	5
I am my emotions	1	2	3	4	5
I feel these emotions; they must be true	1	2	3	4	5
I can't be creative without intense emotions	1	2	3	4	5

Part 2: Write down two myths you have about your emotions and how you struggle with them.

. . . .

. . . .

RAIN, a mindfulness tool

Dr Tara Brach and several other Buddhist teachers designed a new mindfulness tool, RAIN, to help people work with intense and complex emotions.[26] The RAIN steps guide us to change a painful moment and strengthen our capacity to come home to our most profound truth. The mindfulness practice brings a new openness and calm to our daily lives.

RAIN is an acronym for:

- **Recognize** what is happening.

- Allow life to be just as it is.
- Investigate inner experience with kindness.
- Non-identification/Natural awareness.

RAIN meditation is a powerful spiritual tool for cultivating compassion in the face of difficult emotions, limiting beliefs, and conflicts with others. Through the acronym RAIN, we can awaken the qualities of compassion—a mindful presence, caring, and an inclusive heart. RAIN redirects the process in which you resist your moment-to-moment experience. It doesn't matter what pattern you use to fight "what is." RAIN helps to undo these unconscious patterns.

- *Recognize what is happening:* Recognition is the first step by focusing on thoughts, emotions, feelings, and sensations that arise right here, right now. For example, you might recognize the urge to pick up a drink/drug. On the other hand, when gripped by anxiety or anger, you might realize the underlying belief that triggers this physical response. "What is happening inside me right now?" Be curious.

  Imagine you are getting ready for an event you've been looking forward to for a long time. Your friend calls and tells you they have to cancel at the last minute—something urgent came up—but to have fun without them. When they hang up, you notice you're now incredibly uncomfortable and feel very anxious. What's wrong? Then you realize: you don't want to go by yourself—it was always the plan that you two would go together!

- *Allow life to be just as it is:* Let it be. Discover your thoughts, emotions, feelings, and sensations. Allowing is integral to healing and is a conscious intention to "let it be." For instance, when you feel anxious, say "yes" to your experience or "I consent." With permission, whispering a phrase like "yes" softens the hard edges of your pain. Resistance lessens. Over time your defenses relax. You'll choose to "ride the waves." Riding the waves is the practice of riding out your own powerful emotions, observing the experience without trying to force or change it. Although it seems counterintuitive, accepting painful emotions allows for freedom from suffering.

- *Investigate inner experience with kindness:* Sometimes, doing the first two steps of RAIN is enough to reconnect you with your inner self. Not long ago, I realized I was upset by a text I received. My breathing was shallow. I placed one hand lightly on my stomach and allowed myself a deep inhale and exhale. I got a glass of water and relaxed onto the couch, resting my head back against a pillow, taking some more deep, focused breaths.

- *Non-identification/Natural awareness:* Non-identification means your emotions, sensations, or stories do not define you. The first three steps of RAIN require activity. In contrast, this last part of RAIN is a realization that arises independently. Love and compassion are what we need to heal our suffering and the suffering of others. We each have the capacity for love and compassion, but we need to develop it in our daily practice.

ACTIVITY: RAIN

RAIN is a mindful tool for dealing with emotions. Reflect on a situation you would like to address.

Describe the situation.

. . . .

. . . .

. . . .

Recognize the underlying emotion in this situation.

. . . .

. . . .

. . . .

How did you accept the emotion within you?

. . . .

. . . .

. . . .

Now, investigate the emotion further.

List your physical sensations:

. . . .

. . . .

List any thoughts that rise up:

. . . .

. . . .

Putting it all together

In this chapter, we looked at the DBT skill of interpersonal effectiveness, FAST. Self-respect effectiveness teaches us to ask for what we want and need while respecting our values and their influence to shape our priorities. We worked on disproving several common myths about emotions that stop us from leading an emotionally healthy life. We defined and reviewed different types of thought distortions—irrational thoughts that can negatively influence emotions.

We also learned that using the FAST tool helps develop self-respect effectiveness. This particular skill enables you to balance your needs with another person's. Finally, RAIN is a skill for learning how to cultivate the qualities of self-compassion and caring.

By doing Step Four, we peel away a layer of the onion and get closer to our core. Each layer represents denial, the disease of addiction/alcoholism, our character defects, and the harm we've caused. Our soul is at the core of our true selves, our clean and sober selves. A common goal in recovery is to have a spiritual awakening, and by doing Step Four, we move closer to this goal.

Chapter 5

Step Five: Integrity

In this chapter:
→ Stage 2 of DBT
  - Activity: Step Five
  - Activity: Practice of Step Five
→ GIVE skill
  - Activity: Using the GIVE skill
→ DEAR WOMAN skill
  - Activity: Getting what you want
→ PLEASE skill
  - Activity: Practicing the PLEASE skill
→ Visual affirmations
  - Activity: Self-affirmations

Step Five	The DBT translation
Step Five is about speaking openly and honestly about your struggles with substance use with a focus on how you harmed yourself and others	We use the DBT skill of interpersonal effectiveness by learning social skills to be assertive, listen, and attend to relationships

Completing Step Four was tough. Feelings of resentment, anger, fear, hurt, and sadness emerged. However, working through this Step prepared me for Step Five. By sharing my list of assets and liabilities, I was able to see through my blind spots, find out what was true, where I was misguided, and what areas I needed to work on.

Stage 2 of DBT

Stage 2 begins to focus on emotional expression: how to convey emotional experience through verbal and non-verbal behavior.[27] Emotional expression means expressing feelings such as anger, sadness, fear, disgust, surprise, and joy. Only when Stage 1 dangerous behaviors are under control, and you are committed to recovery, do you progress to Stage 2 of DBT.

Each stage focuses on identifying the specific aspects of your behavior that get in the way of your learning, growth, and healing, and you become ready to let them go. In Stage 2, the idea is to bring you out of trauma or neglect. It also means committing and being content with steady improvement. Having flaws does not mean you are defective; rather, it is coming short of where you want to be.

Beginning to tackle the issues deep down, underneath the addictions and dangerous behaviors, is where lasting change occurs. Making an effort to heal the underlying, core, mental, and emotional issues can reduce our destructive behavior. Making a change is not easy, but it is possible. Breaking down behaviors into bite-size pieces makes them less overwhelming. It's essential to keep a sense of humor, and don't forget about Rule 62: Don't take yourself so damn seriously!

In Stage 2, the most common destructive faults to address include chronic despair, involuntary thoughts, suppressing painful emotions, avoidance of situations/experiences, emotion dysregulation, and self-invalidation.

Targets for Stage 2 of DBT[28]

Dysfunctional state	Behavioral target
Chronic despair	Normative emotional experiencing and expression
Involuntary thoughts	Mindfulness of current experience
Suppressing painful emotions	Capacity for emotional experiencing
Avoidance of situations/experiences	Engagement in meaningful activity
Emotion dysregulation	Capacity for emotional tolerance
Self-invalidation/self-hatred	Self-validation/acceptance

As we proceed with Step Five, in addressing our shortcomings, the Stage 2 targets are useful to remind us what we are working toward.

Step Five is about disclosure. Bill W. tells us it's not enough to discuss your shortcomings with your higher power alone. For example, we have seen people in history who were convinced that their higher power directed them to take a particular action. Unchecked by other human beings, this usually had disastrous consequences. Bill W. also mentions that discussing our shortcomings, resentments, fears, etc. can be done with more than one person.

I spent several hours going over my Step Five with my sponsor and therapist. I found the combination of talking to both another alcoholic and to my therapist beneficial. One without the other would not have been enough. My sponsor helped with the Twelve-Step program, and my therapist helped me better understand how my bipolar disorder and depression has affected me and others.

When I read off my list of resentments, assets, values, and secrets, a surprising thing happened. Suddenly, I realized how much resentment I had towards my bipolar disorder! Being hospitalized, experiencing relationship difficulties, employment issues, and how it had all affected my recovery—I was in tears trying to explain this to my sponsor. It wasn't until doing my Step Five that I realized how heavily my bipolar disorder weighed on me.

By quieting my mind's negative self-talk, I felt love—a love for myself I hadn't felt before, and a forgiveness of self. When I heard my sponsor say, "You are loved just the way you are," I took a deep breath in, and tears welled up in my eyes.

I acknowledged my resentments and identified their consequences. More importantly, I admitted my part and found forgiveness. Step Five, for me, was the gateway. I don't see how I could have maintained honesty with myself and with others if I hadn't purged my resentments, resulting in peace of mind. My thoughts had been lying to me. Discussing my darkest secrets gave me my life back.

Telling our story

Many of us have never had the opportunity to tell our story. Telling your life story to your sponsor can be very healing; they'll listen attentively, caring very much about what you have to say. Sharing your story can also be a humbling and liberating experience. A burden lifts. You might not even appreciate the freedom that has been granted to you until you have been able to digest everything. Telling your story, in a way, validates your life. If you're like me, you probably don't feel like you are worthy enough to have someone listen to your story, but you earned your seat and you belong as much as the next person.

Step Five can also be a very stressful process. Step Four forces you to look back at your past destructive behaviors, and Step Five brings it all out into the open, exposing everything and pushing you to be vulnerable. It is natural to feel tender and defensive. The remainder of my Step Five moved forward from that moment.

The following activity can help you break down Step Five to its core: admitting to your higher power, yourself, and a confidant the nature of your mistakes.

⊕ ACTIVITY: STEP FIVE

We admitted to our higher power (of our own understanding).

How does your connection to your higher power help you share your Step Five?

. . . .

. . . .

. . . .

How does turning your life and will over to your higher power help you work Step Five?

. . . .

. . . .

. . . .

Admitted to ourselves...

How have you acknowledged and accepted the exact nature of your mistakes?

. . . .

. . . .

. . . .

Admitted to another human being...

What is the challenge, and what is the gift, of sharing your secrets with someone else?

. . . .

. . . .

. . . .

⊕ ACTIVITY: PRACTICE OF STEP FIVE

In Step Five, we admit our shortcomings, accept our past, and, as a result, try and live a life of integrity, trust, and courage. We seek forgiveness and acceptance to move past our mistakes.

How did sharing your Step Five help you better understand trust, integrity, courage, acceptance, and forgiveness?

. . . .

. . . .

. . . .

To what extent have you developed love and compassion for yourself and for others?

. . . .

. . . .

. . . .

Reflections
What are the consequences of postponing your Step Five?

. . . .

. . . .

. . . .

What tools of self-compassion are you using to be able to forgive yourself?

. . . .

. . . .

. . . .

How have you become more honest with yourself and with others?

. . . .

. . . .

. . . .

GIVE skill

Let's take a look at a new skill that focuses on interpersonal effectiveness and helps us better fulfill our needs and desires, establish healthy boundaries, and form and maintain healthy relationships. Effective communication is a skill that can only be sharpened through daily practice. It is not easy, particularly when you are emotionally distraught. In this case, the GIVE skill in DBT is a simple tool that helps you focus on maintaining and improving your relationships while being efficient in your interactions, regardless of the situation.[29]

You can accomplish this by checking in with yourself and asking:

1. Is your tone gentle and considerate, or is it agitated and harsh?
2. Are you asking, or are you demanding?
3. Are you listening to the other person, or are you interrupting them?

Now, let's break down the skill further:

- *Be Gentle:* You can do this by consciously checking your tone of voice to make sure you are not being aggressive or attacking the other person. Be prepared to accept "no" as an answer. Try to focus on calmly getting your point across instead of using threats or anger to persuade the other person.
- *Maintain Interest:* In order to have a pleasant conversation, express interest in the other person and what they have to say. By show- ing nterest, you are allowing reciprocity and creating space for them

to meet you halfway. Through your body language, facial expressions, and verbal cues, you can demonstrate that you're actively listening and hearing what they have to say. Maintain eye contact, engage in the conversation, and put any screens away. You don't have to fake interest, but practicing these cues can help you become a better listener.

- *Validate:* In the context of relationships, validation means that you are acknowledging the other person's point of view without casting judgments and attempting to rectify what you perceive as a problem. When you validate someone, don't force your opinions onto them; instead, focus on listening to their needs. This skill can be useful when you have disagreements during conversations, as it can show that you acknowledge what they are saying, and helps strengthen your relationships.

- *Have an Easy manner:* In your difficult conversations with others, try to find humor in them when appropriate. It can be challenging to do so, but the more tense the conversations are, the more strain they can cause to your relationships. So instead, practice half-smiling and having an easy-going tone. That can help smooth things over and prevent the conversation from going off the rails.

⬇ ACTIVITY: USING THE GIVE SKILL

Identify a situation where you are working to maintain the relationship and communicate with the other person in a gentle, effective manner. The objective is to lower your emotional reactivity; focus on maintaining the relationship, and both your needs and the other person's. Now reflect on how you used the GIVE skill.

How were you *Gentle* with the person? Any attacks, threats, or judging?

. . . .

. . . .

. . . .

How effectively were you able to use this skill?

Not effective | Somewhat effective | Very effective | Extremely effective

What did you do to let the other person know you were *Interested*?

. . . .

. . . .

. . . .

How effectively were you able to use this skill?

Not effective | Somewhat effective | Very effective | Extremely effective

How did you *Validate* the other person's feelings, wants, difficulties, or opinions?

. . . .

. . . .

. . . .

How effectively were you able to use this skill?

Not effective | Somewhat effective | Very effective | Extremely effective

How did you use an *Easy* manner?

. . . .

. . . .

. . . .

How effectively were you able to use this skill?

Not effective | Somewhat effective | Very effective | Extremely effective

DEAR WOMAN skill

DEAR WOMAN—sounds like the beginning of an email, right? However, it is also an acronym for a skill or strategy taught in DBT. I benefitted immensely from learning the skill of DEAR WOMAN. When I'm struggling, communication can be especially hard for me. DEAR WOMAN is an interpersonal effectiveness skill that helps me work more efficiently in my relationships with others. I use it on a regular basis. It's a skill to communicate more effectively in your marriage, relationships, friendships, and at work.

The first part of the skill is about active communication with someone:

- *Describe* what it is you want. What is your intention or what do you want the result to be?
- *Express* yourself. Be vocal about your thoughts and feelings.
- *Ask* for what you want.
- *Reinforce* others. Positive feedback is crucial! "Thanks!" goes a long way.

The second part is about looking inward and focusing on your behavior:

- *Willingness* to tolerate not getting what you want.
- *Observe* what is happening inside and around me. How am I feeling now? Angry? Sad? Frustrated?
- *Be Mindfully* present in the current moment. Right here. Right now.
- *Appear* confident. Sounds easy, but it is *hard*.
- *Negotiate* with others. Be prepared to meet somewhere in the middle. When emotions are running high, it's hard to remember to use this tool. That's okay—there are other tools you can use. If you're feeling overwhelmed, for example, take a deep breath (highly recommended at all times) and/or say, "I need a break."

In a particular scenario, some skills will be more useful than others. For example, appearing confident and tolerating not getting your way is likely more useful at work. Recovery can feel overwhelming at times, which is why it's more important than ever to be able to communicate your needs effectively.

⊕ ACTIVITY: GETTING WHAT YOU WANT

In difficult situations, use DEAR WOMAN.

Describe the situation.

. . . .

. . . .

How did you *Express* yourself?

· ·

· ·

What did you *Ask* for?

· ·

· ·

What did you do to *Reinforce* the other person?

· ·

· ·

How *Willing* were you to tolerate not getting what you want?

· ·

· ·

What did you *Observe* is going on around you and inside yourself?

· ·

· ·

How are you being *Mindful* and staying in the present?

· ·

· ·

How are you *Appearing* confident?

· ·

· ·

How are you *Negotiating* with others?

. . . .

. . . .

PLEASE skill

It is all too easy to feel overwhelmed by intense negative emotions, which allows your Emotion Mind to take control. Neglecting to take care of yourself both mentally and physically harms your emotional vulnerability. It makes you more susceptible to engaging in negative coping skills, lashing out at others, and responding impulsively. The DBT skill PLEASE is intended to help you reduce emotional vulnerability.[30] It is easier to manage your emotions when you live a balanced lifestyle and create a healthy space for yourself.

PLEASE is particularly useful when working Step Five because rehashing your past to move forward leaves you vulnerable. It can help build resilience while making tough decisions and managing your emotional sensitivity. Let's take a look at how the PLEASE skill works.

- *Treat Physical iLlness:* Pay attention and listen to your body. Your emotions are not just thoughts; they also manifest in physical form. Focus on resting and taking care of yourself when you are sick. Don't skip medication prescribed by your doctor. Schedule regular and routine checkups to make sure you are taking preventive measures as well.
- *Eat balanced meals:* Prioritize your nutritional needs. Practice mindful eating by incorporating fruit and vegetables into your diet and eating food that satisfies and sustains you. Try to moderate the amount of sugar and high-fat food you consume to have a good balance.
- *Avoid alcohol/mood-altering drugs:* Drinking and drugging can impair your judgment and make you more emotionally vulnerable. Use only medications prescribed by your doctor in the recommended dosage. When you feel the urge to drink or use drugs, think it through.
- *Get a good night's Sleep:* It is essential to practice good sleep hygiene to get a healthy night's sleep—anywhere between 7 and 9 hours. Some vital tips could be avoiding screens at least 30 minutes before bed, and going to bed and waking up at the same time every day.
- *Make time for Exercise:* Moderate physical activity for at least 20 to 30 minutes of your day can have profound benefits. Start small—it could be walking your dog around the neighborhood or playing with your

kids at the park. Exercise is proven to be highly beneficial, mentally and physically, as it triggers the release of dopamine and serotonin, brain chemicals responsible for improving mood.

Getting mental exercise is equally important. A great place to start is doing one activity a day that makes you feel confident, capable, and accomplished, no matter how small the task. You can build your confidence every single day by simply practicing it. Set a new goal for yourself so you can measure your growth in a positive, uplifting way.

ACTIVITY: PRACTICING THE PLEASE SKILL

What are you doing to maintain your physical health?

. . . .

. . . .

How is that helping your emotional wellness?

. . . .

. . . .

How are you practicing mindful eating? List *two* examples.

. . . .

. . . .

How are you practicing good sleep hygiene? Has this helped in achieving a better quality of sleep?

. . . .

. . . .

What changes can you make to include exercise in your daily life?

. . . .

. . . .

Visual affirmations

Visual affirmations are another DBT skill. You might think of this skill as giving yourself a pep-talk; for example, "I am beautiful," "I am thoughtful," "I make time to exercise." Reinforce it by repetition and visualization.

This might sound silly, but it works. Essentially, saying affirmations creates new pathways and associations in your brain. Thus, our self-talk is a self-fulfilling prophecy. Be aware, however, of negative language that overpowers an affirmation; for example, "I'm a bad test-taker" or "People don't like me." Develop positive affirmations that describe current behaviors, thoughts, and attitudes that support the affirmation.

Here are some guidelines for creating affirmations:

- Use the present tense.
- Use action words.
- Be positive (state what you want, not what you don't).
- Be specific.
- Be realistic.

Many examples of affirmations are available. Effective affirmations should be specific to you and your goals. Here are just a few:

I walk with determination and confidence.
I hold my head high.
I am strong, physically, mentally, and emotionally.
I live a healthy, positive lifestyle.
I like myself, and people like me.
I am loved and supported by people who are important to me.
I am a loving and caring person.
I am proud of myself.
I am glad to be alive.
I have confidence and poise.
I live by my positive choices.
I accept myself for who I am.
I am intelligent.
I am resilient.
I make wise choices.

ACTIVITY: SELF-AFFIRMATIONS

Using the guidelines and examples above, write down one self-affirmation a day tailored to your own goals and desires.

. . . .

. . . .

. . . .

. . . .

. . . .

. . . .

. . . .

Putting it all together

I truly believe being adaptable in the face of changing circumstances is a sign of good mental health. This means acting, thinking, and feeling in effective ways. Stage 2 of DBT begins to focus on effective emotional expression.

Step Five is challenging to do, but using the DBT skill DEAR WOMAN, focusing on interpersonal effectiveness and emotion regulation, helps you communicate more efficiently in your relationships with others. Skills like PLEASE and GIVE teach you how to be assertive while being gentle, to lower your emotional reactivity, and to focus on maintaining relationships while understanding the other person's needs.

The gift of Step Five is that our relationships begin to change with ourselves, other people, and a higher power. Each step you complete in the AA/NA program, you make a deeper dive into your commitment to the program and recovery. Getting a sponsor, working the steps, finding a home group, taking a service commitment, and going to meetings—each of these actions keeps us on a path of freedom and a new way of living.

Chapter 6

Step Six: Becoming Ready

In this chapter:
- Activity: Step Six
→ Radical Acceptance revisited
- Activity: Radical Acceptance—accepting reality
→ Wise Mind 2.0
- Activity: Wise Mind
→ STOP skill
- Activity: STOP skill
→ IMPROVE skill
- Activity: IMPROVE the moment

Step Six	The DBT translation
Step Six is about removing what doesn't work in your life anymore	We use the DBT dialectical skills of Radical Acceptance and Wise Mind

After completing Step Five, you can clearly see your self-centered, dishonest behavior and attitudes. In her article "Nothing to (im)prove," the famous Buddhist teacher Pema Chödrön says, "Meditation isn't about becoming a better person but befriending who we are."[31] So, who am I? To arrive at this truth takes a lifetime.

Step Six focuses on accepting your character defects exactly as they are and then being willing to let them go. "Defects of character" does not mean you are a defective person. Instead, let's look at your faults and mistakes as shortcomings, coming short of where you want to be. Your defects may rear their ugly head time and again, like a game of whack-a-mole, but it's essential to have patience. Remind yourself that you're doing the best you can.

Understand that this is a commitment to change and that it takes time. It is a step of willingness, the spiritual principle associated with it.

In the process of doing Step Six, I became exhausted. I was trying to do my higher power's part in my spiritual growth and healing process. My part was "being entirely ready"—ready to let my higher power be in the driver's seat. My higher power's influence flowed through my life when I quit trying to control everything.

Readiness allows our higher power to reach into our lives and uncover and remove the things that make us spiritually and emotionally unwell. Thus, the "both/and" in DBT is the doorway to effective change of specific lifelong habits. Our shortcomings block our ability to experience the love, relationships, and the life we want. Once we become aware of these blocks, we can begin to change. It's not easy, though. Keep an open mind and a positive attitude!

⊙ ACTIVITY: STEP SIX

List *two* of your shortcomings, and briefly describe each.

. . . .

. . . .

. . . .

For each shortcoming, describe the ways they affect your relationships.

. . . .

. . . .

. . . .

Choose *one* aspect of your life: what would it look like without these shortcomings?

. . . .

. . . .

. . . .

It is critical to remember that you are human after all. We all need many life skills to manage our character flaws and work toward radical self-acceptance.

Radical Acceptance revisited

In this Step, we revisit and expand on the concept of Radical Acceptance. When you accept absolutely everything about yourself and embrace your life with purpose and intent, you can step out from insecurity and move forward.

Dr Tara Brach states: "Clearly recognizing what is happening inside us, and regarding what we see with an open, kind and loving heart, is what I call Radical Acceptance."[32] When we are in difficult or stressful situations, our bodies tend to tense up. Practicing Radical Acceptance reduces those impulses.

The first phase of Radical Acceptance is to recognize the realities of our experience—the good, the bad, and the ugly—without interfering. Compassion, the second side of Radical Acceptance, is our ability to relate tenderly and sympathetically to what we perceive. The combination of these two helps to guide us by providing clarity and balance in accepting ourselves. By bringing both sides together, we create our own path and take back control of our narrative.

When practicing Radical Acceptance, remember the following key points:

- *You are worthy.* You can learn Radical Acceptance by taking the first step of practicing mindfulness. Next, make building compassion towards yourself and others a daily practice.
- *Allow yourself to feel pain.* When you experience pain, use Radical Acceptance to master how you want to respond. Instead of suffering, recognize the cause of the pain and work on ways to overcome it.
- *Be kind to yourself and to others.* While this is not easy, work on forgiving yourself. First, treat yourself how you would treat a dear friend—with compassion, kindness, and love. Now extend that sentiment to those you meet in your life. Recognize that making mistakes makes us human. When you forgive yourself for your mistakes, you build the capacity to forgive others for the same. However, you don't have to accept unacceptable behavior.
- *Learn to pause.* This is an integral step in Radical Acceptance. A skill I've learned to practice is stepping back from a challenging situation and revisiting it with a relatively calmer sense of self.
- *Redefine your boundaries when it comes to accepting yourself.* Often, the limitations you impose on yourself are of your own making. These may include prejudices, fears, presumptions, and opinions that govern your life rather than help it improve. So, allow yourself to make decisions based on self-acceptance rather than fear.

- *Pay attention.* This is a significant part of being mindful. Observe and remain in the present moment. Become aware of your surroundings, people close to you, and yourself. Notice how you're feeling, how things affect you, and what you have in common with others.
- *Find your refuge.* Find a community that resonates with you and shares your interests. Community helps foster a sense of belonging. It could be a yoga class, a book club, or even your local AA/NA chapter; form a close-knit community of people you can trust.
- *Prioritize your relationships.* It doesn't matter if you are introverted or extroverted, it would be best if you had solid relationships with people with whom to embrace life. You can find true joy in loving others and being loved.

ACTIVITY: RADICAL ACCEPTANCE— ACCEPTING REALITY

What does the word "acceptance" mean for you?

. . . .

. . . .

. . . .

Write *two* things that you have trouble accepting right now.

. . . .

. . . .

. . . .

Out of these two things, are there any facts that you need to accept as reality (vs. a judgment or opinion)?

. . . .

. . . .

. . . .

Write down *two* thoughts and feelings you are having right now.

. . . .

. . . .

. . . .

What tools can you use to help you accept how you're thinking and feeling in this moment? List *two*.

. . . .

. . . .

. . . .

Wise Mind 2.0

DBT uses the concept of a Reasonable, Emotion, and Wise Mind to describe a person's thoughts and behaviors. Logic rules the Reasonable Mind, feelings drive the Emotion Mind, and the Wise Mind is a middle ground between the two.[33]

I rarely acted from a Wise Mind before I joined a DBT group. I primarily functioned from an Emotion Mind. Everything and everyone seemed to "trigger me." People who loved me told me I was too sensitive! Behaving this way did not make me happy, balanced, peaceful, or have healthy relationships. I was an emotional reactor, not a Wise Mind responder.

Wise Mind is a grounded, gut instinct, space within. It was a space I didn't realize I had, and often failed to use. So how did I learn to function from a Wise Mind? Through developing a meditation practice, being mindful in the present moment, and accepting reality without delusion and judgment. I learned that a Reasonable Mind needs an Emotion Mind to become a Wise Mind. This state of mind in DBT is calm, collected, balanced, and capable of making decisions with both reason and emotion.

Everyone struggles with emotions. Paying attention to those emotions is how you learn to manage them mindfully. Wise Mind is about intentionality that you put into the practice of living mindfully. During this process, you train your mind to evaluate emotional states and embrace the good, the bad, and the ugly.

What are some things that can divert you from the path of a Wise Mind?[34]

- Focusing too much on the past or the future
- Being overly critical or judgmental about yourself
- Clinging to specific thoughts and conclusions
- Living without intention
- Having no compassion for yourself and others.

ACTIVITY: WISE MIND

Now, let's focus on these barriers and break down your thoughts in a Reasonable Mind and an Emotion Mind and see how to use both sections to work on your Wise Mind. To know how to respond to challenging situations, you must learn how to use the Wise Mind by reflecting on your Reasonable Mind and Emotion Mind.

Think of a challenging situation you are facing at the moment. Under a Reasonable Mind, write down all the facts you observe, without judgments and feelings

Under an Emotion Mind, write down all your thoughts and feelings about this situation.

Now, reflect on both these sections, combine them in a balanced way, and write down how you can achieve a Wise Mind.

Reasonable Mind	Emotion Mind

Wise Mind

STOP skill

It is human to feel shame and guilt for our past mistakes. It takes effort to move forward and to let a higher power remove our defects. A helpful DBT tool to use in this situation is the STOP skill.

This practical yet straightforward skill can help you in a bind, especially when your emotions are overwhelming and out of control. This skill comprises four steps: **S**top, **T**ake a step back, **O**bserve, and **P**roceed mindfully.

- *Stop:* The first step is to come to a complete halt! This may seem obvious, but it is easy to forget to pause when emotions are triggered.
- *Take a step back:* Walk away from the situation and get some distance. Take some deep breaths to center yourself.
- *Observe:* Now picture yourself as a bystander who has come across this situation. How would they perceive it impartially and without prejudice? When you're observing, pay attention to how you feel physically and mentally—notice how your body tenses up, how your thoughts race, and where they're going.
- *Proceed mindfully:* You may notice a drop in the edge of your emotions after working through the first three actions of this skill. If you're still agitated, reach out to a loved one, meditate, or take a walk and proceed with intention.

⬇ ACTIVITY: STOP SKILL

Think of a situation that is triggering you and try to apply STOP.

First things first, *stop* what you're doing. Now, *take a step back* from the situation.

Observe: Why are you agitated? Write down the thoughts and feelings you are having right now.

. . . .

. . . .

Picturing yourself as a bystander looking at the bigger picture, write down *two* facts about this situation (leave out any opinions).

. . . .

. . . .

If your friend was going through a similar situation, what advice would you give them?

. . . .

. . . .

What do you need to do to face this situation?

. . . .

. . . .

IMPROVE skill

We rarely have control over unpleasant events that occur in our lives. The level of distress we feel can range from losing your favorite pen to breaking up with a loved one. IMPROVE helps us tolerate the pain caused by these different situations. Although strong emotions do not last forever, our actions and the consequences of those actions may have long-term repercussions. As a result, learning the DBT skill IMPROVE is beneficial in tolerating difficult emotions. It is an effective acronym to remember to build your mental and emotional strength:

- *Imagery:*
  - Visualize a better scenario than the one you're in right now.
  - Visualize the precise details of the place.
  - Assume this place is your Wise Mind and consider how you would successfully deal with your problem in this ideal world, where everything is going well. This state of Wise Mind will assist you in dealing with your situation effectively.
- *Meaning:* What springs to mind when you hear the phrase "live with intention"? When you think about leading a meaningful life, what values, thoughts, and actions come to mind? Consider these factors, as well as your purpose, and the significance of what you are going through. Finally, consider what you can learn from those circumstances and how they can help you on your path to sobriety.

- *Prayer:* When you are in an unfavorable situation, try to be mindful, use a mantra, and repeat your favorite prayer. The beauty of prayer is that, just like your higher power, it does not have to be rooted in religion. Instead, focus on yourself, connect to your higher power, and surrender.
- *Relaxation:* When you are distressed, your body physically tenses up. Engaging in techniques such as deep breathing, stretching, yoga, and body scans can help you relax and relieve some of the pressure and tension built up. To do a body scan, pay close attention to each part of your body and their sensation, in a gradual sequence, from your head to your toes. It is easier to calm your mind when you are physically relaxed.
- *One thing in the moment:* Learn to focus on one thing at a time. Mindfulness is a tool for slowing down and taking time to be in the present moment. Concentrate on your breath, sensations, and thoughts, one at a time. Being present directs your attention to the here and now rather than the past or the future. Find a single task to accomplish and work on it with intention; this approach will help you feel less overwhelmed.
- *Vacation:* This does not have to mean packing up and running off to Aruba. It simply means taking a break. As with any holiday, the goal is to temporarily leave your troubles behind and go to an ideal place. Then, add some fun and excitement to your routine by doing something you don't normally do. Do the same thing by catching up with some friends or going for a walk outside. Eventually, when you are ready, you'll be able to return to the problem with a clearer mind and tackle it with greater ease.
- *Encouragement:* Work on being your own cheerleader. In times of need, you don't always need external validation; it can come from yourself. It's incredible to have your own back. When assessing the situation, be realistic, and give yourself genuine encouragement to hold on to hope and get through it. To keep your spirits up and know that you can get through the situation and come out the other side, remind yourself, "This too shall pass" and "I got this!"

ACTIVITY: IMPROVE THE MOMENT

Think of a current situation that is unpleasant, out of your control, and causing you distress. Now, let's use IMPROVE to work on making this situation tolerable.

Imagery

Describe a safe place.

. . . .

. . . .

List *two* good things or memories that you are proud of.

. . . .

. . . .

Meaning

Reflect on the situation that is out of your control. Find purpose or meaning in it. What is it?

. . . .

. . . .

What are you learning from this?

. . . .

. . . .

Prayer

What are you holding in mind as you pray?

. . . .

. . . .

List examples of when your higher power has entered your life and answered your prayers or the prayers of someone you know.

. . . .

. . . .

Relax

List *two* ways of relaxing, e.g., breathe deeply, give yourself a massage, take a hot bath, do yoga, etc.

. . . .

. . . .

Practice one of the above. How effective was this exercise in helping you relax?

Not helpful | Somewhat helpful | Helpful | Very helpful | Extremely helpful

One thing in the moment

What grounding skills are you practicing when distressed?

. . . .

. . . .

Pick *one* exercise: Sing a song—notice your breath and feel the vibration of sound. Body scan—pay close attention to each part of the body, one at a time; notice any sensations or tension that you may be holding. Change surroundings—move to a different setting; if you're alone, maybe find somewhere more populated.

How effective was this skill?

Not helpful | Somewhat helpful | Helpful | Very helpful | Extremely helpful

Vacation

List *two* things you could do on this vacation, e.g., go to the beach, woods, park, etc.

. . . .

. . . .

Once you come back from this vacation, reflect, and write down how you feel.

. . . .

. . . .

Encouragement

Write down *two* cheerleading statements you can tell yourself when you are discouraged.

. . . .

. . . .

Putting it all together

Step Six begins with acknowledging that we are fallible. But by accepting ourselves, warts and all, we can let go of our shortcomings from a place of self-love. With Radical Acceptance, we can see the multifaceted nature of our traits and can address them with compassion. By extending the principle of Radical Acceptance to our broader reality, we can cultivate a Wise Mind: Reasonable Mind and Emotion Mind working in harmony. By strengthening our Wise Mind through a practice of mindfulness, we become adept at making decisions free of judgment, with both reason and emotion.

The STOP skill implores us to pause mindfully before responding, instead of reacting, and the steps in IMPROVE are beneficial for tolerating difficult emotions.

Chapter 7

Step Seven: Humility

In this chapter:
→ What your ego says vs. what your higher power says
→ Stage 3 of DBT
  - Activity: Step Seven
→ Dependence and independence
→ A being mind and a doing mind
  - Activity: Being, doing, and balancing
→ Walking the middle path to a Wise Mind
  - Activity: Dialectics
  - Activity: Walking the middle path

Step Seven	The DBT translation
Step Seven is about removing your shortcomings and replacing them with humility	Courage is needed to reflect on our values and build on our character strengths by working the DBT skill of walking the middle path

Walking the middle path to a Wise Mind, in DBT, is like wearing a jacket that protects us from the outside elements. But wearing a jacket can only protect us from the outer world. Mindfulness protects us from both the outer and inner worlds. We are protected from the outer world because we can see it more clearly and from the inner world by being mindful and aware of how we react. In addition, mindfulness strengthens our ability to act with kindness. Working the previous six Steps, we've stripped away age-old layers of denial, ego, self-centeredness, and other shortcomings that consumed us when we were active in our disease.

Step Seven is about removing our shortcomings and replacing them with humility and spiritual principles. It involves a personal transformation of ourselves. Asking our higher power to remove our shortcomings is only half the job. First, we need to change our behavior. Then, we need to start looking at how we can contribute to others in the world. My mother once shared with me: *When one door closes, another one opens*. I had to give up the life I knew to live the life I hoped for.

Humility means having a balanced perspective of ourselves. In AA/NA terms, it means being "right-sized." Before recovery, our thinking was very black and white. We were either a piece of s#!t or the best thing since sliced bread. In Step Seven, we realize that we are neither; we are on the middle path.

What your ego says vs. what your higher power says

What your ego says	What your higher power says
I'm a victim of chance	I write my own story
I only have one life, and it's very scary	I only have one life, and that's okay! I will take it one day at a time
I compete with the world	I am at peace with the world, so I don't need to compete with the world
I have no more energy to give	There is an abundance of energy to draw from around my higher power and me

We ask our higher power to remove our self-entitlement, grandiosity, shame, regrets, and unworthiness. You've already taken your very first act toward humility by admitting your powerlessness and unmanageability. Humility is accepting "life on life's terms."

Step Seven is an ongoing opportunity to gain humility as an aspect of staying clean and sober. It takes work to stand up for ourselves, be patient, or tolerate the emotional discomfort of new behaviors. Likewise, gaining awareness of our shortcomings and responding instead of reacting takes work. As you gain an understanding of your shortcomings, you'll soon start to trust your gut and intuition; for example, what am I feeling? Do I need to pause for a moment?

Whenever we react, it's important to reflect on it and change it, either with a DBT skill, AA/NA tool, or by talking with a therapist, sponsor, or friend. We are all part of one another. We may not look anything alike, but we are all on the journey of recovery together.

Stage 3 of DBT

The aim of this stage is to solve everyday problems while improving happiness and joy in day-to-day life. The first two DBT stages offer new ways of behaving. Slowly, you begin to live free of the mind, body, and soul's reckless chaos, and make changes from those harmful habits. By taking accountability in solving life's problems, you're building new traditions and rituals—new brain maps to help you develop a practice of control over your habits and behaviors. In addition, behaving in new ways enables you to understand the weight of childhood trauma, neglect, and abuse.

This stage in DBT focuses on owning your behavior, building trust in yourself, and learning to see your innate value. Being familiar with DBT now, as someone also in recovery, you are moving forward. The first two stages have offered you new ways of behaving. You have started to live free of that dangerous, frantic chaos of the heart and mind, and have begun to change those destructive habits.

Targets of Stage 3 of DBT

Dysfunctional state	Behavioral target
Familiar state of sadness and depression	Improving happiness and joy
Blaming others for your behavior	Focusing on your side of the street
Not trusting your gut feelings	Building trust in yourself
Comparing and despairing	Learning to value yourself

Putting Step Seven into action can mean saying "no" when a friend asks you for a ride because you don't have time. "Into action" can also mean setting a boundary, pausing when agitated, and practicing restraint of tongue, pen, email, and text. Likewise, interacting with people, places, and things that trigger you. Now, let's break down what you'd need to work this Step.

ACTIVITY: STEP SEVEN

What does "humility" mean to you?

. . . .

. . . .

How do you prepare when asking your higher power to remove your shortcomings?

. . . .

. . . .

How do you "surrender"?

. . . .

. . . .

List *two* times when you didn't act on a shortcoming and practiced a spiritual principle instead.

. . . .

. . . .

List *two* shortcomings that have been removed from your life.

. . . .

. . . .

Dependence and independence

Dependence is a challenging concept for me. I want to be independent in my daily life, but I realize I cannot get through all of the challenges life brings on my own, without my recovery community and my higher power. However, the reality is that relying on a higher power requires enormous strength and courage, and only makes you more independent. As a consequence, dependence on a higher power is indeed a means of achieving true spiritual independence.

When optimizing for self-preservation and safety, many of us have concluded that it feels like the better choice not to express even a hint of "weakness" or emotionality for fear of being taken advantage of, invalidated, or disrespected. For some of us, it comes from family, for others, classmates, but wherever it starts, it tends to spread. Soon, we don't know how to tell even our partner or closest friends when they hurt our feelings or do something that crosses a line. Before recovery, I didn't feel safe being vulnerable in front of others. I was afraid of being ridiculed, put down, and laughed at.

However, after I got clean and sober, I quickly realized that the weight of my fears, limitations, insecurities, and worries was too much for me. My back was against the wall, but I still did not want to admit my vulnerabilities to others or to God. It was easier for me to stay firm on the outside, but that wall had its cracks. As a child, I learned to bottle up my emotions for survival. In recovery, my feelings began to seep through the cracks. This is how the healing begins.

But why would I give up the wall I had built around me? Because shoving my feelings down had begun to chip away at my core and break my resolve. When I shared my emotions or prayed, I took a concrete step of letting down my walls. I started to trust by opening up to my therapist and sponsor.

By being dependent on God through prayer, I was able to admit my vulnerabilities and begin to deal with them in my daily life. I finally felt comfortable acknowledging them aloud among friends and sharing them in interactions with others. I also began to see the power of being dependent on a higher power. I found refuge, healing, and security as I learned to be vulnerable and trade my emotional independence with a dependence on God.

By allowing myself a dependence on a higher power, I let something new into my life: faith. Faith requires only to open yourself, through willingness, to acceptance. Through acceptance of God and God's wisdom, I realized my wisdom alone was not enough, as any alcoholic or addict can attest to. It did not bring me to a safe, secure, fulfilled place. Self-will run riot is a recipe for conflict and even disaster. However, many of us fear that any dependence weakens us, takes away our control, and harms us in the long run. On the contrary, once we begin recovery, we face the fact that we have more problems to address than just our addiction. Something must have led us here, down this path, in the first place.

By exercising our will and making decisions over our lives that were entirely our own, we did not end up happier, better off, or more fulfilled. Maybe we thought so at first, or perhaps we can pretend, assisted by foggy memory, but we were not well. That is why we are in recovery!

And yet, we cannot address all our other problems with a quick fix either. We have placed our faith in AA/NA, our sponsor, and our friends, but these supports can only hold so much of our insecurities, doubts, and fears.

While becoming more dependent on my higher power, I learned how to balance my independence and dependence on others. A community was something I longed for; however, due to being bullied throughout childhood, I was wary around groups. But by embracing the experience of unconditional love and support from a higher power, I no longer feel the need to compete for the attention of my peers or compare myself to others who, much to my frustration, held the power to make me feel incompetent, devalued, or "wrong."

Instead, with the support of my higher power—and some curiosity—I began to experience people in recovery as patient and kind, even though I often resisted their support. I felt my walls coming down when I started to accept the love freely given from the Twelve-Step community.

A being mind and a doing mind

It's all too easy to persuade ourselves that the more we accomplish, the happier we'll be. We could go on an endless quest to ponder on all our shortcomings. But how do we get out of that loop of either doing nothing or aggressively pursuing our goals, to live a life worth living?

Research has shown that we have a limited number of core activity patterns in the brain, and they correspond to our most fundamental states of mind: being and doing.[35] A being mind, in DBT, is defined as the mental state in which we are present, allowing ourselves to experience joy while being aware of ourselves. In this state of mind, instead of constantly striving for the next accomplishment, we make peace with ourselves, our progress, and our achievements.

Dr Marsha Linehan describes a being mind as a "nothing to do mind." Contrary to this is the doing mind, where we are focused on moving from where things are at the moment to where we want them to be. We can stay in a being mind and fixate on our desires, but they will not come to fruition unless we take actionable steps to achieve them. In a doing mind, we are aware of the present moment, but are compelled by our desire to move closer to a goal.

It is possible to become trapped in the never-ending, unsatisfying pursuit of being in one of two modes, where you are either stagnant in your position or always on the lookout for happiness around the next corner. A Wise Mind is the perfect balance between the two modes, and you are centered and conscious, working actively toward your objectives.

How does understanding the balance between the two and working towards achieving a Wise Mind help during Step Seven? Achieving a balance of a being and a doing mind enables you to acknowledge your goals and take steps to work on them.

Now, let's take a look at how we can use this DBT skill to balance these modes of mind.

How do you know which mode of mind to engage?

- A being mind: Visualize where and how you want things to be.
- A doing mind: Compare that image to your current view of how things are.
- A being and a doing mind: Now, think of steps you'll need to take to get there.

⊕ ACTIVITY: BEING, DOING, AND BALANCING

Consider a goal for how you want to feel today.

. . . .

. . . .

. . . .

List *one* skill that will help you achieve that goal.

. . . .

. . . .

. . . .

Once you've used that skill, how has it made you feel?

. . . .

. . . .

. . . .

In the table below, write a few examples of a being mind, a doing mind, and how you can achieve a balanced Wise Mind.

Being mind (mindful, accepting, and focused on the present)	Doing mind (driven, analytical, goal-oriented)	Balanced Wise Mind (focused and aware while working on your goals)

Walking the middle path to a Wise Mind

Walking the middle path requires swapping out your black and white thinking with the dialectical thinking pattern of "both/and." As we've learned before, black and white thinking is a typical alcoholic or addict trait where you have an all-or-nothing perspective. For example, you might believe that you will never get sober or that relapse is inevitable.

Being stuck in these extremes causes more harm than good as they exaggerate reality and cause suffering. In addition, you risk being out of balance and invalidating other possible avenues of thinking instead of making room for compromise.

There is always a balanced view of a situation that you can train yourself to focus on instead. Developing that ability is walking the middle path. You can recognize your shortcomings by being self-aware and accepting a higher power's need in this state. Step Seven focuses on pursuing humility as a practice and foundation for a life worth living. Learning and applying this skill of walking the middle path is a powerful tool that can guide you in working this Step.

How do you use this skill? Walking the middle path aims to achieve a state of peace, contentment, and open-mindedness where we stop thinking in extremes. To reach these goals, the fundamental thing to work on is thinking in dialectics—accepting that two opposites can be true.

Here are some examples of dialectics:

- You can be self-sufficient and also need help.

- You can be content alone and also crave a connection with others.
- You accept yourself as you are and you also want to change and grow.
- You can disagree with someone and still love and respect them.
- You can understand someone's motivations and still disagree with them.
- You can say "no" and still have a relationship with others.

ACTIVITY: DIALECTICS

Write down a few statements that are dialectics.

· ·

· ·

· ·

· ·

The key takeaways to walking the middle path are:

- *Validate yourself and others.* In any circumstance, when you are communicating with another person, read the signals they are giving—their body language, reactions, and feelings towards the current situation. Notice if these signals are in line with the problem at hand, and then consider their perspective. Be open-minded by acknowledging their responses. This approach does not equate to agreeing with them.
- *Get some perspective.* There is always another side to the story. Look at it from your perspective and from the other person's, and then remove yourself from the situation and look at it from an unbiased third perspective as an outsider. Disagreements don't have to mean the end of a relationship because you can both agree to disagree.
- *Accept change.* Prepare for adversity and change so that when they occur you are emotionally and mentally prepared to handle them with ease. The middle path is a happy medium between accepting a situation and changing it.

ACTIVITY: WALKING THE MIDDLE PATH

Use this activity to reflect on different situations and how you chose to walk the middle path.

Think of a situation you are going through at the moment. List *one* way you can choose to walk the middle path.

. . . .

. . . .

. . . .

Where were you in relation to the middle path?

Accepting.. ↑..Changing

Doing mind.. ↑..Being mind

Think of another situation. List *one* way you can choose to walk the middle path.

. . . .

. . . .

. . . .

Where were you in relation to the middle path?

Accepting.. ↑..Changing

Doing mind.. ↑..Being mind

Putting it all together

In Step Seven we focus on removing our shortcomings by practicing humility and spiritual principles. This involves a personal transformation of ourselves. Asking a higher power to remove our shortcomings is only half the job. We also need to change our behavior. Building trust in yourself and learning to value yourself are the main Stage 3 targets of DBT. Patience is necessary; gaining awareness of our shortcomings takes time.

A being mind is defined as the mental state in which we allow ourselves to experience joy while in the present moment. In this state of mind, we make peace with ourselves, our progress, and our accomplishments. In a doing mind, we are aware of the present moment and compelled by our desire to move closer to our goal.

Step Seven is a practice and foundation for a life worth living. Learning and applying this skill of walking the middle path is a powerful tool that will guide you in working on this Step. There is always a balanced view of any situation. Being open-minded to someone else's responses does not mean you agree with them; it means you're open to both sides. Remember to validate yourself and others, and don't forget—perspective is the middle path!

Chapter 8

Step Eight: Willingness

Step Eight	The DBT translation
Step Eight is identifying the harm you have caused others and listing those names	We do some soul searching and identify those we harmed by using the DBT skills of interpersonal effectiveness that help build assertiveness and accountability

Making a list means identifying the relationships where you've caused harm. By making a list and putting down names, it takes the power out of guilt and shame. I wrote a moral inventory in Step Four; now, in Step Eight, I needed to examine situations differently. I worried: would those people I'd harmed be upset? Would I follow through? What if the other person wouldn't listen? What if they rejected me? Future-tripping interfered with the task at hand. My sponsor's advice was simple: make the list. It meant focusing on the here and now, on the details. What specifically did I do, and to whom and when?

There was no coming back from Step Eight. Once I recognized the harm,

I could never un-see the fallout. But, on the positive side, I moved forward without the weight of guilt and shame. Although fear got in the way many times, I held my head high and my heart open.

⊕ ACTIVITY: CATEGORIZING YOUR STEP EIGHT LIST

Return to the list of people from your Step Four inventory, which includes friends, coworkers, and family members. In Step Eight, we prepare to address the harm we caused. The goal of this Step is to overcome isolation due to our behaviors. "Making a living amends" means to live a new lifestyle. With a living amends, you commit to making genuine improvements for yourself and others, including following a sober path. You do not need to apologize explicitly, but you must make up for the harm you caused and endeavor to repair that relationship in other ways. We will discuss this and other types of amends in more depth in the next chapter.

Who was harmed?	Make amends? (Yes, No, Not yet)	Make a living amends?
My partner	No	Yes
Coworker	Yes	Yes

Building mastery

It is entirely possible to feel stuck or stagnant in our recovery if we are not progressing. This feeling is normal. I have often felt stuck, unmotivated, and even trapped in a negative space. In recovery, our confidence wavers and may eventually drop. Even the most mundane tasks can seem complex and overwhelming.

In times like this, the DBT skill of building mastery is invaluable to have in your toolbox. This skill helps build confidence and self-esteem, which tend to take the biggest hit during a slump. When you feel capable and self-assured in your abilities, it is easier to go through life with confidence. Don't hesitate or shy away from trying for the fear of failure. The purpose of the building mastery skill is to reinforce a positive outlook toward trying new things. It moves you away from the inner dialogue that sets you back, from "I'm not capable of that" or "I can't do it" to "I can do this" and "I am capable and worthy."

Building mastery facilitates this shift by helping you engage in small, routine activities that make you feel confident, in control, and capable. When you consistently do things that boost your self-esteem and confidence, encountering something bigger or less favorable has little to no impact. You won't make the common mistake of abandoning something when faced with a challenge. Instead, you set small goals that allow you to step out of your comfort zone.

Reflect on the standards you set for yourself and deem acceptable. Would you expect the same from a loved one? Would you cut them some slack for making mistakes, or would you judge them?

Let's examine the facts behind limiting assumptions we hold. In the table below, write down a few judgments and consider how to reframe them.

⊛ ACTIVITY: REFRAMING JUDGMENTS

Judgment	Why do you think that?	Positive reframing
I am not good enough	I think and feel this way when I'm feeling insecure about my capabilities	I am worthy even when I make a mistake

Once you've dissected the standards you set for yourself, let's move on to the larger goal of working on tasks that can aid you in regaining your footing.

Here are a few pointers before we do the following activity:

- This skill is about doing small, challenging things regularly.
- This skill will reinforce your confidence, competence, and sense of control.
- Focus on setting achievable, bite-sized goals that also challenge you.
- Appreciate the efforts you are making.

⬇ ACTIVITY: BUILDING MASTERY

Make a list of some activities that give you a sense of mastery.

. . . .

. . . .

. . . .

. . . .

Choose *one* activity to try. What activity did you choose, and why?

. . . .

. . . .

How did working on this activity make you feel?

. . . .

. . . .

Building mastery allows you to focus on day-to-day things that can build your capacity to accept, have a sense of control, and reduce your vulnerability, rather than the possibility of failing to make a list. When working on Step Eight, it's tough to focus on the task of making a list of people we've wronged. It is an emotionally charged task that can dredge up many resentments, anxiety, and shame about the past from which you are trying to move forward. To do so, we must first learn to accept the past.

Attending to relationships

Love is never a safe bet. The main ingredient of love is vulnerability. When we are vulnerable with someone, we become open to love. The more connected we are to other people, the happier we feel. We are lifted by our moments of connection and shared enjoyment with our loved ones.

Our relationships include with family, friends, groups, and communities. Maintaining connections with our colleagues, friends, and a clean and sober community gives our life meaning. Our resilience builds our relationships with other people. Creating and maintaining these relationships is not always easy. We might start with a loving, supportive relationship, but stress, lack of attention, and neglect can take their toll, causing possible conflict. AA/NA is one community built up around a primary purpose: to help the alcoholic or addict who still suffers. Still, people can get sidelined into infighting and scapegoating, and may become divisive. As a result, we can end up feeling like an outsider, hurt, and upset.

Relationships take courage and strength. Therefore, it is essential to attend to and nurture our relationships with the important people in our lives and to strengthen the communities to which we belong. Two significant pitfalls in maintaining close personal relationships are neglect and not dealing constructively with conflict. Attending to your relationships, even when you don't feel like it, is the way to keep them happy, supportive, and personally satisfying:

- *Take time:* Spend time with a partner, children, family, and friends regularly. One-on-one time is best.
- *Be present:* A significant challenge is not being fully present. During the time spent with loved ones, the number one rule is: *Put down your phone.* If not, the message you're sending is, "The phone is more important than you." It can wait!
- *Express appreciation:* Displays of appreciation nurture relationships. Everyone needs to be appreciated and encouraged, whether these kind words are to a colleague, friend, partner, or child.
- *Listen:* Listening is an essential communication skill. Hearing out the other person's point of view is the first step to resolving any conflict.
- *Learn to communicate:* Our relationships suffer when one or both individuals speak in an aggressive, explosive, or disrespectful way. Learn to talk respectfully and assertively, using the DBT skills FAST (Step Four) or GIVE (Step Five).
- *Make amends and forgive:* All close relationships involve disappointment and hurt at times. Take responsibility and make amends when

you have hurt someone. Forgiving and moving on is key to maintaining relationships through hard times.

As part of an AA/NA community, it is easy to assume that it will always be supportive and there for us; however, just like families and personal relationships, the groups and organizations you belong to need to be nurtured and energized. All groups need leaders and members willing to contribute and give back. People who give often feel even better than the ones they help. You also benefit by becoming more involved in a community and making a difference.

Here are some tips for improving relationships:

- Reflect on the relationships in your life at the moment.
- Are any under stress at the moment? Do any of them need nurturing?
- If so, take action to improve things.

For example, you can:

- Call or check in with a friend you haven't spoken to in a while.
- Send a "thank you" card to a friend, family member, or colleague.
- Listen without judgment to a family member with whom you have conflict.
- Apologize to a loved one.

Conflict resolution techniques

The mere thought of confrontation or conflict might sound scary. Despite this feeling, it is essential to understand how to approach conflicts in a healthy manner, whether you struggle with anger or freeze when being criticized. In DBT, interpersonal skills can help you achieve your goals while focusing on improving your relationships and modes of communication. This particular set of skills is crucial when you are working Step Eight and readying yourself for the next step where you make amends—preparing for both positive and negative outcomes.

When we argue or disagree with someone, it is natural for our bodies to go into fight or flight mode, and our Emotion Mind can take control. To avoid that state of mind and communicate more healthily, let's look at a few strategies that could help.

- *Validate each other:* When we previously worked on the DBT skill GIVE (in Step Five), we briefly discussed the topic of validation. A common denominator in many conflicts is not feeling heard or validated. People stop listening because they do not feel heard. Mutual validation can help break the cycle and enable you to get your message across while also understanding the other person's perspective. This approach does not imply that you agree with their point of view or dismiss your own. Instead, you tell them you recognize how they feel, even if you don't agree.

- *Broken record:* When your message simply isn't getting through to the other person, make a brief and understandable statement to rectify the situation. The sentence should clearly state your desire without going into detail about why and what you need. Using this skill, maintain your assertiveness and repeat yourself as necessary, to avoid engaging in a fruitless debate.
- *Probing:* This skill is valuable when you need to get to the bottom of a situation where the other person disagrees. Inquire, "What is it about this specific circumstance that bothers you?" This question usually opens up the conversation to uncover the root of the issue, especially if it is unclear.
- *Finding a middle ground:* Also known as "clouding," with this technique, you partially accept what the other person has to say.[36] Identify a statement the other person is making that you agree with, and use it as a starting point to avoid escalation, to instead find common ground. When emotions are running high, you can use this strategy to shift the focus to what you mutually agree on and even out the playing field.
- *Intentional pause:* When things begin to spiral out of control, take a step back and give yourself some space. Process the situation, calm yourself, and return with a more balanced and rational approach. The STOP skill is a more in-depth version of this approach (see Step Six).

While you cannot control or predict how other people will react, you are always in control of your behavior. You have the power to control how you respond to challenging behaviors and situations. You can combine one or more of these strategies into action steps using the following DBT skill, THINK, to help solve conflicts more effectively.[37]

THINK skill

This particular DBT skill moves you away from Emotion Mind and helps you reach a Wise Mind.

Let's break it down:

- *Think:* Consider the situation from the other person's perspective. Try and put yourself in the other person's shoes to examine how they may interpret your words and actions. This approach will allow you to see their side and validate them, even if you disagree.
- *Have empathy:* Be empathetic to the other person's emotions and thoughts.
- *Interpretations:* Every situation has many perspectives. Be open to seeing these perspectives. Consider alternative possibilities, with a focus on reaching at least one positive outcome.
- *Notice:* Take note of how the other person is contributing to the situation. How are they attempting to resolve the problem? How are they demonstrating that they care about this? Are they dealing with personal issues that may have an impact on this situation?
- *Kindness:* Always do your best to treat others with kindness. Treat others the way you would want to be treated yourself.

⬇ ACTIVITY: USING THE THINK SKILL

Describe a situation and how it is upsetting you.

. . . .

. . . .

Now put yourself in the other person's shoes. How is their perspective different from yours?

. . . .

. . . .

What do you think the other person might be feeling?

. . . .

. . . .

Can you think of other reasons for their behavior?

. . . .

. . . .

Has the other person indicated they want to resolve this situation? How?

. . . .

. . . .

Have you been kind to the other person during this disagreement?

. . . .

. . . .

Clarifying priorities in Interpersonal relationships

Clarifying priorities is an essential interpersonal skill in DBT. It is critical to be aware of your goals in interpersonal situations. It is especially crucial to have a plan for discussions involving conflict, business, and other pressing subjects. The ability to clarify priorities is essential when dealing with other people. Sometimes, when emotions are hot, we lose focus and veer off track of our goals in the exchange.

How solid is a relationship if a person denies their own needs for the sake of the relationship? Although a person can survive in such a relationship for some time, frustrations will build up. Denying our needs usually breeds resentment. The sense of inequity is extreme, and one of two things will happen: the frustrated individual will either blow up, or, in frustration, leave the relationship. Either way, the relationship comes to an end or is in serious jeopardy.

Deciding which effectiveness skill to use

We have previously worked on the DBT skills of FAST, DEAR WOMAN, and GIVE—they all correspond to different types of effectiveness. Consider all three types of effectiveness in every situation with a specific interpersonal objective or goal:

- Objective effectiveness (DEAR WOMAN; see Step Five)
- Relationship effectiveness (GIVE; see Step Five)
- Self-respect effectiveness (FAST; see Step Four).

Each of these types of effectiveness may be more or less applicable in a given situation.

1. What is *one* thing you've done that lowered your sense of self-respect?

    . . . .

    . . . .

2. What are *two* things you've done that increased your sense of self-respect?

    . . . .

    . . . .

3. Which one of the effectiveness skills would you most like to master?

    . . . .

    . . . .

ACTIVITY: CLARIFYING PRIORITIES IN INTERPERSONAL SITUATIONS

The effectiveness of a behavior in a situation depends on a person's priorities.

Example 1: Objective effectiveness
The goal or intention of the interaction, which is often a tangible outcome, is referred to as "objective effectiveness." For example:

- *Situation:* Polly believes her landlord kept her damage deposit unfairly.
- *Objective:* Get the deposit back (most important to Polly).

- *Relationship:* Keep the landlord's goodwill, and get a good reference (second most important).
- *Self-respect:* Not lose respect by getting too emotional, "fighting dirty," or threatening.

Let's discuss a situation and identify the objective(s) in the problem, the relationship issue, and the self-respect issue for each case. What is your priority for the situation?

Situation:

. . . .

. . . .

Objective:

. . . .

. . . .

Relationship:

. . . .

. . . .

Self-respect:

. . . .

. . . .

Example 2: Relationship effectiveness

Relationship effectiveness represents the goal of a conflict-free relationship. For example:

- *Situation:* Margot's best friend wants to come over and discuss a problem; Margot is tired and wants to go to bed.
- *Objective:* Go to bed.

- *Relationship:* Keep a good relationship with the friend (most important to Margot).
- *Self-respect:* Balancing caring for her friend with caring for herself.

Let's discuss another situation and identify the objective(s) in the problem, the relationship issue, and the self-respect issue for each case. What is your priority for the situation?

Situation:

. . . .

. . . .

Objective:

. . . .

. . . .

Relationship:

. . . .

. . . .

Self-respect:

. . . .

. . . .

Example 3: Self-respect effectiveness

Self-respect effectiveness is maintaining or improving your respect for yourself and respecting your values and beliefs. For example:

- *Situation:* Rosie wants a raise, but her boss continually overlooks her achievements.
- *Objective:* Get the raise; establish a boundary.
- *Relationship:* Gain the boss's respect and goodwill (second most important to Rosie).

    − *Self-respect:* Not violate her self-worth by settling for her current pay (most important to Rosie).

Can you think of times you have risked losing what you want at work or sacrificing your self-respect for a short-term gain? Examples may include attacking another person for voicing criticism, demanding to get your way, not doing your best, etc. List *one* circumstance where you risked your wants, needs, and self-respect for short-term benefits.

. . . .

. . . .

How did you feel after taking that risk?

. . . .

. . . .

Putting it all together

In this chapter, we looked at what Step Eight means. First, we made a list— what specifically did I do to whom, and when? We also learned the DBT skill of building mastery, which helps build your confidence and self-esteem. The purpose of this skill is to reinforce a positive mindset when trying new things.

We realized that the main ingredient of love is vulnerability. When we are vulnerable with someone, we become open to love. Attending to relationships is also a critical DBT skill. The more connected we feel, the happier we are. Clarifying priorities is another essential interpersonal skill. It's necessary to be aware of your goals and plan for discussions involving conflict, business, and relationships. In DBT, interpersonal skills help you achieve your goals.

Chapter 9

Step Nine: Taking Responsibility and Making Amends

In this chapter:
→ Types of amends
→ Spiritual principles of Step Nine
  - Activity: Making amends
→ Cope Ahead skill
  - Activity: Coping Ahead
→ Interpersonal effectiveness scripts
→ Recovering from invalidation

Step Nine	The DBT translation
Step Nine is about making amends and repairing relationships	We continue to use the DBT skills of interpersonal effectiveness—specifically, analyzing problem interactions and coping with conflict, which assists in communicating more effectively when making amends

Working Step Nine restores our balance. In Step Nine, I made direct amends to those I had harmed. Our sponsors can help us determine when and to whom to make amends. We admit and accept the limitations placed on us by unfinished business from the past. When we feel stuck due to fear or guilt, we can remove it through positive action. Amends allow us to repair the rupture.

I also made indirect amends by paying back the debts I owed, I wrote letters, and I apologized. At times, my negative self-talk was overwhelming, followed by feelings of shame and guilt. It took insight, courage, and dedication to make amends. Luckily, I had the help of my therapist, sponsor, and a higher power.

At this point, we are on our way to a happier, more functional life. We have committed to staying clean and sober. In addition, we have put our faith in a higher power. DBT skills such as mindfulness and interpersonal effectiveness have supported us on our journey. As a result, things are getting better because we are less willing to engage in destructive behaviors.

Doing Step Nine takes courage, patience, self-awareness, and good judgment. Step work is cumulative, with each Step preparing us for the next. It allows us to change the way we feel about our past and to repair relationships. Although guilt and shame can weigh us down, when we begin to transform them, we move closer to freedom.

Finally, we understand what it means to make amends. Making amends is not the same as making an apology, although an apology is one way of making amends.

Types of amends

There are three different types of amends that we can make:

- *Direct amends:* Usually, when we talk about making amends, we are referring to direct amends. To make direct amends is to speak (or write) to the people we have harmed. But, of course, this won't always be possible. For example, you may need to make amends to someone who is now deceased, or perhaps to someone you have no current contact information for, despite your efforts to track them down. After making direct amends to my high school principal, he said a job was waiting for me when I finished college! On the flip side, when I made amends to a teacher, he proceeded to add, "and don't forget you also did this and this." I was taken aback. We have no control over how other people will respond.
- *Indirect amends:* We can find a way to right the wrongs of the past (even if direct amends are not possible) through volunteering, making donations, or, more generally, finding ways to help others. For example, I made amends to different department stores by sending $10 (what I could afford at the time) every month, with Step Nine written on the amends letter inside, and no return address.
- *Living amends:* When we live our lives respectfully, honestly, and with dignity, we show ourselves and others our commitment to change. Living amends start when we begin changing and continue long after speaking directly to someone we have harmed. Living amends also means following an emotionally sober path. The AA/NA phrase

"emotionally sober" means that we are capable of facing our problems and addressing them in healthy ways without the aid of substances. It's vital to achieve emotional sobriety—otherwise, the same stressors that drove us to drink or to use drugs will propel us in that direction again.

We don't need to keep looking over our shoulders. We don't have to cringe, be a doormat, or invite attacks with our vulnerability. Instead, we mend the links and build bridges with other people. Repairing a relationship then creates a change in others' attitudes towards us. The person they meet in us is different.

Lastly, many of us find it helpful to reflect on our amends after making each one. We can do this by writing about it, having a conversation with a sponsor or therapist, or sharing about it in a meeting.

To keep things as simple as possible, keep these three concepts in mind during Step Nine—the "three Rs" of making amends: restoration, resolution, and restitution:

- *Restoration* means returning something to its previous state, undoing the harm done. For example, we may be able to restore trust in the context of a relationship. We can also restore our relationships and our career by making amends.
- *Resolution* involves healing past experiences that are still hurting or disturbing us in some way. We look for solutions that allow us to lay these experiences to rest. For example, we may be holding on to hurtful words spoken or actions taken by our caregivers when we were children. Finding resolution can mean developing understanding or compassion for those who harmed us and for ourselves.
- *Restitution* relates to Step Nine by returning something material (or abstract) to its rightful owner. Paying off debt is an excellent example. The truth is that each day that we make an effort to refrain from hurting others—and instead practice kindness—is a day when we've practiced our living amends.

When deciding when to make amends, each situation is different. There are some people we ought to make amends to as soon as possible. There are other cases when it might be better to wait. Then there will be situations where we are better off not making direct amends at all, choosing instead to focus on indirect or living amends. You can reflect and decide how best to handle each situation.

Once you have identified the people to whom you will make amends and when, you will need to think about how you will do it. It also helps to have some idea of what you're going to say—having a plan keeps you anchored to your true intentions in making amends. Finally, it's essential to let the other person know your intentions to see if they are ready to have that conversation or not.

Lastly, your sponsor can help you check your motives for telling people about your addiction or offering apologies. You may want to ask yourself how much that person needs to know, and if you do want to go forward with the interaction, what purpose will be served by your self-revelation.

Dealing with rejection

No one likes the feeling of rejection, but when we make amends, we don't know how we are going to be received. So, it's essential to turn over the outcome to a higher power. Making amends can inspire us to change our behavior.

Making amends, particularly direct amends, requires emotional maturity and good communication skills. In addition, we will need to draw on what we have learned in previous Steps to handle these interactions skillfully. Otherwise, there are many traps we could fall into, including blaming others or shaming ourselves.

Spiritual principles of Step Nine

In Step Nine, we focus on the spiritual principles of humility, forgiveness, and love. We gain humility through taking a good look at the damage we have done to others (and to ourselves) and accepting responsibility. Being forgiven is a beautiful feeling, and it can inspire us to forgive as well. Being forgiven reminds us of others' capacity for compassion, and makes us aware of the good intentions people have. Finally, love is a core value—we practice loving ourselves and others. We focus on empathy rather than blame, and on recognizing the good in all people, including ourselves. Love is inherent in all of the Steps, but it stands out in Step Nine.

Lastly, we need to continually apply what we are learning, one day at a time. Step Nine is a lifelong practice, but as long as we are willing to continue integrating it into our lives, we can maintain our freedom.

⊕ ACTIVITY: MAKING AMENDS

In this activity we clarify the advantages and disadvantages of making our amends.

People I have harmed	Potential benefits of making amends	Potential hurt caused by making amends

Now that we have looked at the concept of making amends from a Twelve-Step perspective, let's see what DBT has to offer us in the way of skills that will help us with Step Nine.

Cope Ahead skill

As we have discussed, we don't know what kind of reactions we will get when we make amends. Therefore, the Cope Ahead skill can help us prepare for the potentially stressful outcomes we may face.

The Cope Ahead skill can interrupt a cycle of destructive behavior. It allows us to practice what to do if we find ourselves facing that situation, and to develop a plan ahead of time. To master this skill, we must be honest with ourselves. As we practice this skill, we will become more adept and our responses to such situations will improve. Let's break down how we can use this skill.

Identify the problematic situation(s)

The first step to using the Cope Ahead skill is to reflect on the kinds of situations that have typically tripped you up. For example:

- *Addictive or compulsive behavior:* We all know how difficult it is to stop the cycle of addiction once it starts. When we Cope Ahead, we examine the behaviors that our addiction causes. We need to be fearless when we reflect on this, taking an honest look at the times we have fallen into destructive patterns.

- *Emotional instability:* You can use Cope Ahead to deal with situations that may cause you to explode in frustration, fear, or hurt. Rather than repeating old ways of reacting, this skill can be a tool to help you change. For everyone, the trigger situations will be different. That's why each of us needs to identify what sets us off.
- *Procrastinating and avoiding:* If you struggle with avoidance or procrastination, this practice can help you understand why you avoid taking action or making decisions. Remind yourself "Avoid avoiding" to keep from putting things off or not facing situations that cause you discomfort. Confronting these situations will actually reduce anxiety and minimize problems overall.

When to use the Cope Ahead skill

The Cope Ahead skill takes time to learn and practice. Looking inside when emotions are not running high presents an advantage: we can tap into our Wise Mind. As we learned before, a Wise Mind is the synthesis of a Reasonable Mind and an Emotion Mind. Generally, our best decisions come from a Wise Mind. Sometimes, there's a very brief moment in which we think, "I might regret saying or doing this." But then our Emotion Mind takes over and we say or do it anyway, only to regret it.

The Cope Ahead skill helps guide us in planning an effective strategy. That way, we have a fighting chance of changing even our worst habits. I recommend getting support with practicing Coping Ahead.

Finally, make a plan to change your behavior

Identifying the situations that trip us up is only the beginning. The next step is to make a plan. Harness the power of your imagination to rehearse each situation, or ask a friend or family member to role-play a scenario.

Use the Cope Ahead skill when you anticipate being in a stressful or problematic situation. Making amends is an obvious example of a stressful situation, but here are some other conditions that might trigger anxiety, insecurity, frustration, negative self-worth, etc.:

- Family get-togethers
- A party with people you don't know
- Traveling
- Losing your cell phone

- Taking a test
- Going to the doctor or dentist
- Moving to a new location
- Break-up/divorce.

⬇ ACTIVITY: COPING AHEAD

Describe a worst-case scenario you are worried about at the moment.

. . . .

. . . .

What are some ways you can cope with this scenario?

. . . .

. . . .

List another worst-case scenario you are worried about at the moment.

. . . .

. . . .

What are some ways you can cope with this scenario?

. . . .

. . . .

Interpersonal effectiveness scripts

When we make amends, we draw on what we've learned about interpersonal effectiveness. Interpersonal effectiveness is a DBT module that asks us to consider the kinds of outcomes we'd like to see, and then to consider what actions we can take that will most likely result in those outcomes.

Assertiveness is a straightforward form of communication that is neither passive nor aggressive, and it is one of the central interpersonal effectiveness concepts. When we are assertive, we freely express our hopes and needs without pressuring others to comply. Assertiveness supports you to grow and enrich your relationships, and will help you when making amends.

- *I think:* Be careful not to go on the offensive! For example, "I think you're a jerk" is not effective. Instead, here is an example of how "I think..." could be used in an amends dialogue: "I think that things have been difficult between us, and I take responsibility for my part."
- *I feel:* Once again, be careful not to go on the offensive! For example, "I feel that you bring out the worst in me" is not a good example of an "I feel" statement. It is a judgment and an accusation cleverly disguised as a statement of feeling. Instead, use descriptive feeling words like "hurt," "lonely," "scared," "guilty," "sad," etc. An example of how an "I feel" statement could be used in an amends conversation is, "I feel remorseful about some of my past behaviors."
- *I want:* Here, you get to directly express what you would like to have happened, although be careful of some common pitfalls. For example, "I want you to stop being angry at me" is not a good "I want" statement because you are essentially asking someone to think or feel differently. Instead, ask for specific, measurable behavior. An example of an "I want" statement in an amends dialogue is, "I want you to hear me out, even though this may be a challenging conversation for both of us."

Being transparent and specific about what we want can provoke anxiety, especially if we don't feel we deserve good things or respect. We may not even feel we are worth the effort that we are asking someone else to exert on our behalf. Nevertheless, we are.

Recovering from invalidation

In addition to Coping Ahead and interpersonal effectiveness, recovering from invalidation is a skill we may need to draw on in Step Nine. We have already established that we cannot predict how others will react when we make amends. When we speak from the heart, we make ourselves vulnerable. It may hurt if people respond with anger, mistrust, or resentment, but remember, our past actions likely contributed to those feelings. Therefore, when you make amends, don't let yourself get into an argument.

Now, it is crucial to remember your basic bill of rights as a human.

Your bill of rights

1. You have the right to have needs.
2. You have the right to make requests of others.
3. You have the right to put yourself first sometimes.
4. You have the right to your feelings.
5. You have the right to your own opinions, beliefs, and values.
6. You have the right to your experience.
7. You have the right to speak up.
8. You have the right to ask for help and support.
9. You have the right to say "no."
10. You have the right not to take responsibility for someone else.
11. You have the right to walk away from a harmful situation.
12. You have the right to make mistakes.

What is emotional invalidation?

Emotional invalidation is the experience of having our thoughts and feelings belittled, dismissed, or disbelieved. Invalidation often occurs through words. For example, if you were to share that Step Nine is intimidating for you, and I were to respond, "Don't make such a big deal about it," that would be emotional invalidation. Non-verbal communication can do the same thing. For example, if I rolled my eyes at your admission that Step Nine is intimidating for you, that would also have been a form of emotional invalidation.

Types of emotional invalidation

Let's explore the concept of emotional invalidation more thoroughly. We already know that emotional invalidation can be either verbal or non-verbal:

- *Making assumptions:* When someone assumes how you feel, they may unknowingly be invalidating your experience. You may, in fact, feel quite different, and would have appreciated the opportunity to speak for yourself.
- *Sweeping it under the rug:* When someone tries to comfort you by saying things like "Don't cry! Everything will be okay," they generally mean well. However, what if you need to cry? Furthermore, how do they know that everything will be okay?

How do we know when we are in an invalidating environment?

While each situation is different, invalidating environments tend to have these common characteristics:

- Emotions are often ignored or dismissed.
- Displays of emotions are unwelcome in favor of tight behavioral control.
- Problems are minimized or ignored.

Why do people invalidate others?

Sometimes, we may invalidate one another even with the best of intentions. This can happen because:

- We may not have learned how to validate other people's experiences.
- We may be afraid or uncomfortable with emotions.
- We may want to fix what is wrong rather than simply listening and being supportive.
- We may have underlying feelings of anger or resentment.

How to validate others

Validation has everything to do with active listening. The first and most important step is to pay attention to what the other person is saying. Stop whatever else you might be doing. Don't multitask. Right now, someone needs your authentic presence. Show interest with your expressions and body language.

Now, let the other person know what you heard or observed. State it tentatively, not as a statement of fact, and be open to correction if it wasn't quite right. Be non-judgmental, and don't try to change the other person's experience. Try to keep your tone as neutral as possible. For example: "So, if I understand you right, you're disappointed in me because I was late?"

Coping skills for emotional invalidation

Now that we know what validation and invalidation look like, let's talk about coping when our emotions are invalidated:

- Take a step back and notice your reaction.
- Am I overreacting? Was there any truth/constructive criticism in what was said to me?
- Let go of judgmental self-talk.
- Remind yourself that you and others are doing their best.
- Be compassionate towards yourself.
- Admit whatever sadness or anger you feel about the invalidation.
- Share your experience with a trusted friend or confidant.
- Practice Radical Acceptance.

Putting it all together

Step Nine is about being free—free of guilt, blame, resentment, and self-centeredness. The freedom we experience in making amends is priceless. When we are free, we can live more in the moment, appreciating the people and experiences in our lives. Making amends is by no means an easy thing to do—we put our best foot forward without knowing what the outcome will be. Hopefully it will be a source of connection, joy, and relief.

The skill of Coping Ahead allows us to prepare effectively to prevent sudden emotional distress, such as invalidation. Emotional invalidation means our thoughts and feelings have been belittled, dismissed, or disbelieved. We know that most of us have been guilty of emotional invalidation at some point, and that people can mean well even when they invalidate others. We have learned how to practice active listening to validate others, and we have learned skills to cope with our feelings when others invalidate us. Be kind to yourself as you go about practicing these skills!

Chapter 10

Step Ten: Taking Stock

In this chapter:
- – Activity: Step Ten
- → Chain analysis
- – Activity: Chain analysis
- → Opposite action
- – Activity: Opposite action

Step Ten	The DBT translation
Step Ten is about paying attention to how your actions affect others, and if your efforts were harmful, promptly admit it	Using the DBT skills of chain analysis and opposite action, we identify the cause of past hurts, admit when we were wrong, and tolerate distress

Step Ten is where my recovery started to shine. When I was wrong, I used to explain away why I did or didn't do something. I seemed to have a reason for everything! I assumed if you saw my point of view, you would understand why I made that mistake, so you wouldn't fault me for it. Sometimes, I felt guilty when rationalizing or justifying my behavior. My shortcomings became apparent to me. I became more honest. Rather than leaning into stubbornness, I learned to recognize my mistakes as they happen, so that I can catch them in the moment.

Humility is one action that keeps my side of the street clean. I often forget the benefit I get from receiving feedback. Instead, I tend to let my justifiable mind seem authentic, thinking I know what the next right thing to do is, when all I have to do is look into my past and see when I've deluded myself.

In Step Ten, we focus on cultivating honesty, integrity, and self-discipline.

In recovery, we can think of integrity as sharpening an awareness of which principles to practice in any given situation. Especially when facing challenges or setbacks, holding fast to these principles helps us maintain a strong sense of self and personal pride.

The emotional and negative thought patterns that had led me in the past to drink or use drugs usually stemmed from the impulse to find an easier, softer way through. A lack of discipline led me to indulge in self-serving tendencies rather than pushing myself toward personal and spiritual growth. The only way to strengthen discipline is to practice it, by recognizing the rewards that lie just beyond the hurdle. I call on my inner strength even when old ways of thinking tell me it is useless. For instance, I attend AA meetings even if I'm tired, busy at work, relaxing, or filled with despair. I call my sponsor, work with others, and practice spiritual principles because I am committed to recovery. These actions help assure my continued recovery.

Managing my own needs alongside those of others is a balancing act. In any interpersonal relationship, whether romantic, professional, or platonic, the task of resolving conflicts can be tricky. Being reactive, like raising my voice, only inflames a situation. Instead, looking openly and honestly at my feelings at the moment, acknowledging them, and learning to overcome the urge to block them has reduced my resentments. Now, I take time to act in service of both myself and the other person. I'm committed to greater self-respect and patience. If respect does not flow in both directions in a relationship, however, it may be time to walk away. I take comfort in knowing that I am allowed to keep high standards for how others treat me.

Step Ten affirms the continued importance of taking personal inventory, not only to recognize our wrongs, but our victories, too. By recalling successes that have come from sticking to our values, we can build a framework for behavior that helps us respond better to future situations. In becoming aware of our feelings, we must recognize the specific actions they give rise to—or the actions they don't. The function of Step Ten is to keep us present. Maintaining awareness of our thoughts, feelings, and behavioral motivations—and the links between them—is the only way to reset our patterns consciously.

While it may be hard to admit your mistakes, apologies are a necessary part of life. The truth is that some thoughts, feelings, words, and actions are harmful to yourself and others. Examining and resolving your thoughts and actions each day is an integral part of Step Ten. Trust that practice and patience will lead to continued progress.

⬇ ACTIVITY: STEP TEN

Work on this activity before going to bed every day.

List *one* instance where you were resentful, selfish, or dishonest.

. . . .

. . . .

Have you shared this instance with another person?

. . . .

. . . .

List *one* thing you have done for another person today.

. . . .

. . . .

What did you do today to let your higher power remedy your shortcomings?

. . . .

. . . .

Chain analysis

Chain analysis works by drawing on the events surrounding a particular instance of a specific behavior—more specifically, a behavior that you are trying to change. Seeing how our behavior fits into a broader pattern is the first step toward breaking harmful "chains."

It may seem easy to remember a list of events or recall a situation perfectly. Most of the time, however, the narratives our brains tell us don't provide the most complete or accurate picture. Because it is essential to recognize every step in the chain, we organize the sequence of events into five components. This way, isolating each aspect of the chain becomes much easier, and we can now work to undo these patterns.

The five elements of a chain analysis are:

- Vulnerability factors
- Prompting event
- Links (thought, emotion, behavior, other events involving self and others)
- Target behavior
- Consequences (short and long term).

One time I forgot I had plans with my girlfriend. I woke up to angry voice-mails. Instead of calling back immediately to apologize, I felt shame. As a result, I made myself suffer that whole day. I didn't let myself do anything enjoyable, make other plans, or even eat. Instead, I sank myself into my misery. This negative feedback loop, of course, didn't help the situation. Isolation is never a healthy problem-solving strategy.

One way to conceptualize the chain is like this:

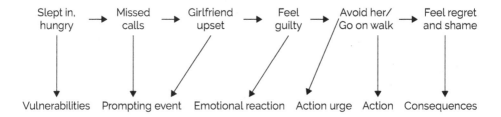

Looking at the situation in a complete chain analysis (see below), it becomes clear to me that there were opportunities to make more constructive decisions at every step in the chain. Making a reasonable assessment of the situation and myself would have significantly helped me to reach a positive resolution.

Order of events	The events that took place	Possible solutions or skills I could apply at this point
Vulnerability factors	Was asleep prior to being alerted of my mistake; woke up hungry	Upon waking, address my physical condition (e.g., drink water, eat toast)
Prompting event	Missed phone calls and angry voicemails from my girlfriend	If I acknowledge her emotions quickly and make amends, I will counter some of the harm I caused rather than avoid the situation altogether

Behavior, emotion, or thought	Thought: Oh my god, I ruined our plans Emotion: Shame, guilt Thought: I'm no good Emotion: Disappointment in myself Thought: I don't deserve my girlfriend Behavior: Got out of bed, brought the phone into the kitchen Thought: Maybe I should try to explain what happened... Emotion: Slight hope	Making a mistake that made someone else unhappy does not negate my innate self-worth. Although I can't undo the past, being honest and understanding will prove my integrity
	Thought: I can't... She will probably just yell at me, and I can't face that Emotion: Fear of confrontation, sadness Thought: There is no way I can fix the situation Emotion: Hopelessness, despair Thought: How could I have messed this up? Emotion: Anger Behavior: Get dressed and leave the house on foot	I can't control people, places, and things—and it's not realistic to try and manage people's reactions all the time. The best I can do is own up to my actions After admitting fault, if the other person holds on to their anger, it's up to them to deal with those feelings If I tell her how bad I feel about everything, she will probably understand, even if she is still mad. I can offer an idea to make up for the plans we missed at another time Maintaining a healthy relationship depends on mutual respect, which means honest communication and being available to make things right
Problematic behavior	Behavior: Avoiding my girlfriend, thereby preventing both of us from being able to process the situation and move past it Behavior: Withholding food from myself	Calling my girlfriend at any point during the day and making a genuine apology for missing our plans and any other harm I caused Getting some food, improving my mood, and likely being in a better headspace to address the situation rationally and calmly

cont.

Order of events	The events that took place	Possible solutions or skills I could apply at this point
Immediate consequences	Immediate thoughts: I must suffer to make up for the suffering I caused. By atoning for my mistakes, I will absolve myself Immediate feelings: Lacking self-confidence, sorry for myself, guilty, hungry Immediate behavior: Going on "a useless walk" all alone just to get out of the house/run away from shame	Practicing the DBT skill of self-compassion, imagine talking to a friend, what would you say?
Later consequences	Later thoughts: It's not going to get any easier to face this problem. I shouldn't have waited so long. She doesn't even know what I'm going through today, and would probably think I'm being stupid. I didn't even think to ask her how she's doing! Later feelings: Further diminished self-confidence, stress, fear, regret, shame	Consciously extending loving kindness to both myself *and* my girlfriend

 ACTIVITY: CHAIN ANALYSIS

Vulnerability factors are dynamics present in your life prior to the incident that contribute to negative thoughts and feelings. For instance, these facts might include a lack of sleep, tension/conflict with a given person or a certain setting, perceived disrespect, etc. They're unfavorable conditions that make us prone to making choices that don't serve us.

When doing a chain analysis of your own experience, recall the problematic behavior in as much detail as possible. This includes thoughts, anything that was said (take note of self-talk as well), and the intensity and duration of the problem behavior. Try to paint a vivid picture. There's no doubt that it's hard to look directly at our failings, but by confronting what led up to these actions, we can seek necessary changes.

Order of events	The events that took place	Possible solutions or skills I could apply at this point
Vulnerability factors		
Prompting event		
Behavior, emotion, or thought (Recall and list as many of these as you can, in the order they occurred; be thorough)		
Problematic behavior		
Immediate consequences		
Later consequences		

You've now learned to recall the dynamics that led you to engage in problematic behavior and to recognize possible risk factors. The following skill, opposite action, is a tool for confronting negative thoughts and feelings while they are still occurring. In addition, this skill encourages us to consider a new way of breaking out of emotional patterns that hurt more than help.

Opposite action

Opposite action is a DBT skill that helps to reframe a situation by purposely reorienting our emotions in a more constructive direction—the opposite of what old habits are telling us. By becoming aware of emotional patterns that don't benefit us, we can shift focus to a more helpful course of action.

In DBT, the opposite action skill is an intentional method for breaking out of your usual emotional response patterns. The following are some ways of applying this technique to common emotional reactions.

- *Fear:* Rather than hiding from a fear or anxiety, confront it on your terms, like a time you know to expect it, or with a friend by your side.
- *Anger:* If you're angry, avoid the person or circumstance that's irritating. Try to consider other perspectives, even if it feels strange to do so, and do not escalate the situation further.
- *Sadness:* Rather than drawing into yourself to ride out the sad feelings in solitude, try making decisions that will get you out of isolation—make plans with others, find an activity you enjoy, or clean your room/apartment/house.
- *Shame:* Running from shame never works in the end. It is better to promptly face the facts to minimize any harm, both for your benefit and for others.
- *Guilt:* If you feel guilty, let yourself experience it. Ask gently for forgiveness, but accept the consequences that come. If the responsibility is disproportionate to the action and doesn't require an apology, try not to dwell on it, and move forward with confidence.

For example, I was heartbroken when a clay pot my daughter made in kindergarten accidentally broke when moving it to clean a shelf. Instead of beating up on myself out of frustration and guilt, I allowed myself to sit with the sadness. I realized this was also an opportunity to pick up the phone and call my daughter, as we hadn't spoken that week.

When a long-term relationship ended, I wanted to stay at home and isolate. However, while my emotions influenced me to stay cooped up at home, the opposite action had me do something different. I told myself to go outside and do something positive instead; I went swimming at the community pool.

Isn't it simply ignoring emotions?

No, it's not. What's vital about opposite action is identifying that you are experiencing a particular emotion in the first place. Having that primary emotional language is crucial for being able to implement opposite actions. However, that doesn't mean you should push down or ignore the emotion. It's more of a simple acknowledgment, which creates distance and separation between your feelings and actions.

Do emotions dictate actions?

Yes, they can. One aim of opposite action is not to let your emotions drive the bus. It's essential to be in a Wise Mind. Many folks believe they don't have control over their emotions. Yet, that's not true. You have the power to choose not to act on your feelings.

"How do you get to Carnegie Hall?"

If you spend enough time around 57th Street and 7th Avenue in New York City, you're bound to hear the joke "How do you get to Carnegie Hall?" The answer—practice!

Opposite action takes practice to see the results—but you don't have to practice alone. By working with a therapist who understands this skill, and other DBT skills in general, you will have a greater likelihood of success. By learning and practicing these DBT skills, making wiser choices becomes possible. Opposite action is a skill that helps reframe a situation by purposely reorienting our emotions in a more constructive direction—the opposite of what our feelings are telling us. By becoming aware of emotional patterns that don't benefit us, we can shift focus to a more preferable course of action.

 ## ACTIVITY: OPPOSITE ACTION

This activity aims to help you see the detrimental patterns in your behaviors when feeling negative emotions, and shows you how it helps to resist the urge to give in to these emotions and take positive steps to promote your mental health and wellness.

Objective: Overcome overwhelming emotions by consciously flipping them, to bring about a better outcome.

Step	Example
1. Recognize the feeling	Fear about moving to a new place Anxiety about the unknown
2. Identify the resulting action	Refusing to think about or make any plans for your move Spending all your free time having fun with local friends
3. Apply opposite action	Do some research online to find potential community involvement, job postings, and other events and opportunities in your new location that you can look forward to
4. Feel the opposite feeling	Excitement and curiosity to try new things and meet new people Relief at being more aware and prepared to take the next steps

Now it's your turn to apply these steps in your life.

Step	A situation in your life
1. Recognize the feeling	
2. Identify the resulting action	
3. Apply opposite action	
4. Feel the opposite feeling	

Putting it all together

In Step Ten, we recommit to the daily practice of taking an inventory. Keeping aware of how we are doing is vital to staying on track in our recovery. Think of this process of self-reflection like being a gardener. Imagine a beautiful, well-grounded tree. You notice some branches here and there that are withering or are bothered by pests: these only steal energy from the rest of the tree.

As you carefully prune away harmful thoughts, emotions, and actions, you let go of the mechanisms you have developed that don't serve you—instead, replacing them with a fuller understanding of managing your behavior in healthy and constructive ways.

We also looked at how holding ourselves accountable for our mistakes makes healthier relationships, both with ourselves and with others. Through being honest about our faults and having the self-discipline to act quickly to right wrongs, we maintain our integrity. We learned to do a chain analysis of problematic behavior, and saw how this skill assists us in isolating individual thoughts, feelings, and actions to our benefit. By focusing on all the events within a singular incident, we can uncover our triggers, vulnerabilities, and thought patterns to minimize future risks.

Now that we recognize patterns that don't serve us or others, the opposite action skill is a method to approach difficult circumstances in more beneficial ways. By applying the opposite feeling and action to what comes automatically, we have more options for responding to a stressor. This skill both pressures and supports us to try something new in service of our best selves.

The activities in this chapter assist in breaking down the components of these skills. Through reflecting on specific occurrences in your life and identifying the potentials for positive change, you will begin to notice how and when to apply strategies that support your goals of integrity, honesty, and self-discipline.

Chapter 11

Step Eleven: Seeking a Deeper Connection Through Meditation

In this chapter:
- Activity: Step Eleven
→ Accumulate positive emotions
- Activity: List of pleasurable activities
- Activity: Accumulating positive experiences
→ Spiritual mindfulness
→ Loving kindness
- Activity: Loving kindness meditation and reflection

Step Eleven	The DBT translation
Step Eleven connects you to a higher power by being mindful, meditating, praying, and paying attention	We explore the common denominator of meditative practice in both DBT and Step Eleven by incorporating the skill of mindfulness and deepening our conscious contact with a higher power

People often approach prayer expecting to become spiritually enlightened immediately, but we usually start from a place rooted in our shortcomings. For instance, we may ask to become a more patient, gentle, forgiving person, and less of a judgmental, reactive, and argumentative person. Anne Lamott confesses, "I would rarely be in conformity with the Divine's huge, crazy love so I just prayed, 'Help me start walking in your general direction,' and the greatest prayer, 'Help me not be such an asshole.'"[38] As in this honest example, it helps to start small and keep it real. We're in recovery because we want to be better people. Now, let's break that sense of purpose down further. What is it we really, truly, want?

In my early recovery, I agonized and asked lots of questions at meetings: about praying, meditation, and what "conscious contact" meant. First, I developed a spiritual practice by reading meditation books. Second, I took the opportunity to deepen my conscious contact through meditation and prayer. My thoughts are my biggest obstacles to meditation. They drift through my head, distracting me, upsetting me. Once I stop paying attention to them and refocus on my breath, I get back to meditating. Third, I put my faith in something greater than myself. By practicing prayer and meditation daily, my relationship with my higher power grew. Fourth, having felt alone a lot in my life, practicing Step Eleven helps me feel less alone.

Later in my recovery, I added mindfulness meditation to my practice. Adopting a formal meditation practice helped me control my thoughts and journey deep inside myself. For example, I talk to my higher power while hiking with my dog, Truffles.

I continue to read books and listen to podcasts that encourage my spiritual journey. All of these habits help me stay centered. My perspective continues to change as my purpose evolves. Love is the highest power around. As the Beatles once said, "All you need is love." We all need love.

ACTIVITY: STEP ELEVEN

Here are some Step Eleven guideline questions that I have found the most useful. These can also be used at various intervals in recovery:

How has your understanding of a higher power changed? List *two* ways.

. . . .

. . . .

How has prayer and meditation helped you put things in perspective?

. . . .

. . . .

List *two* ways you have seen changes in your life as a result of prayer and meditation.

. . . .

. . . .

When do you notice the presence of a higher power in your life?

. . . .

. . . .

Did you pray or meditate today? List *one* action step are you taking to improve your conscious contact with your higher power.

. . . .

. . . .

It's time to put knowledge, faith, and ideals into action; you can't pass on to others something you do not possess. We accept that we're no longer running the show and we let our higher power take the wheel. Letting go of our self-will run riot leads to more satisfaction and success. As part of our spiritual awakening, we begin to manifest the three elements of recovery in AA/NA: the body, the mind, and the spirit. Your past will no longer feel as if it was a waste of life. You will come to realize how adverse experiences can serve a greater purpose. Moreover, you will convey this message to alcoholics and addicts who are still suffering.

Now, we will look at how the DBT skill of accumulating positive emotions can help us deepen our recovery and add to our toolbox.

Accumulate positive emotions

When you accumulate positive experiences or emotions, you learn how to do things that you can participate mindfully in, experience happiness or pleasure, and genuinely enjoy—all without judging yourself or feeling guilty.

With this skill, we make it our goal to partake in enjoyable and satisfying experiences each day, thereby accumulating positive emotions in the short term. We need an outlet for engaging in pleasurable activities. By learning to accumulate positives, we have a more balanced consideration of our emotions and other factors, which will provide both short- and long-term benefits.[39]

"I don't have time for any other activities," you may say. However, even a few minutes can make a difference. It's crucial that when accumulating positive experiences, you do so mindfully. It can be challenging to do things you enjoy when you are stressed out and experiencing negative emotions.

If you can't carve out time, use the activity as a reward after completing any urgent tasks. If negative feelings toward yourself hold you back from engaging in a pleasant experience, try applying the opposite action skill. Instead of avoiding the positive, allow yourself to seek it out deliberately. Think of some enjoyable things and write down at least 5–10 possible activities. Some of mine include playing the guitar, writing in my journal, going for a swim, bike riding, or hanging out with friends.

Here are some other examples:

- Spend time outdoors
- Dance
- Go for a walk
- Go for a bike ride
- Spend time with family
- Call/reach out to an old friend
- Treat yourself to a favorite food
- Go to a museum
- Compliment a stranger
- Spend time with friends
- Take some pictures (get artsy with it)
- Watch a show or movie
- Get a massage
- Listen to good music
- Write in your journal or sketch
- Reorganize your room
- Take yourself on a "date" (e.g., get a smoothie and go to the park).

ACTIVITY: LIST OF PLEASURABLE ACTIVITIES

List some activities that bring you joy.

. . . .

. . . .

. . . .

. . . .

. . . .

. . . .

Accumulating positive experiences helps you work Step Eleven because it rewires ingrained thought and behavior patterns. We gain practice acknowledging and regulating how and when we feed our emotional needs, balancing positive emotions alongside neutral or negative ones. This skill helps build up greater self-confidence in your capability to influence your emotional state in balanced and healthy ways. In addition, knowing you will have that daily positive keeps your emotional reserves from being depleted. The goal of accumulating positive experiences and emotions is to increase your "ups" by making them more frequent and stable.

We acquire positive experiences through both short- and long-term experiences. Like those listed above, short-term activities are essential to making us feel good, and it is necessary (and healthy!) to give ourselves more of those good and happy feelings. Planning our lives so that positive events can arise over a longer span or occur more consistently is vital to what makes life worth living.

ACTIVITY: ACCUMULATING POSITIVE EXPERIENCES

Which pleasurable activity from your list are you working on each day?

Day 1: . . . .

Day 2: . . . .

Day 3: . . . .

Day 4: . . . .

Day 5: . . . .

Day 6: . . . .

Day 7: . . . .

Now, how you felt when doing each activity mindfully.

Day 1: . . . .

Day 2: . . . .

Day 3: . . . .

Day 4: . . . .

Day 5: . . . .

Day 6: . . . .

Day 7: . . . .

Let's return to the concept of mindfulness. This word gets thrown around a lot, but what does it mean, and how can we apply it? First, it is the act of holding your awareness in the present so you can fully experience the enjoyment you deserve from an activity or experience. When a positive experience occurs, we often push it back down on instinct, like a game of whack-a-mole. As a result, our minds fill with looming anxieties and concerns that distract us from the potential of joy. These anxieties have their time and place, but unless you're addressing them then and there, it's okay to let them go. Through continued practice focusing your attention on the present moment, you will train yourself to experience good emotions more frequently and more deeply.

Spiritual mindfulness

Mindfulness is the backbone of DBT, the core skill that underlies all other skill sets. It is the first skill taught in DBT because, without it, the steep road to changing our long-standing patterns of feeling, thinking, and acting is nearly impossible to surmount. Employing mindfulness is central to regulating emotions, getting through moments of crisis without worsening the situation, and successfully resolving interpersonal conflicts. We also invoke mindfulness to access the valuable insight of our Wise Mind.

Overall, mindfulness is considered the basic foundation to becoming wiser, more loving, and more generous. Mindfulness can help us reach freedom from being controlled by our desires, fears, and confusion. Instead, we invoke the potential to move toward more profound connection, clarity, joy, interdependence, empathy, calm, and unconditional love.

A friend suggested, "When you have a thought, just notice it, but let it go, like a cloud in a gentle breeze." Sitting in silence, withholding judgment, and letting passing thoughts and worries float enabled me to feel more centered and honest. I recognized love beneath an ego I held on to like armor. It was an essential step in accepting myself for who I am, who I've been, and all I can be.

With this perspective, I learned to use prayer to keep in touch with my higher power, whom I trust to recognize and remind me of my genuine self. Some of the most recognized features of spiritual practice are interconnectedness, compassion, wisdom, and unconditional love. I became more aware of my place among others and the world.

Mindfulness in spiritual moments can fuel our faith. Faith also fits into mindfulness because it presents an understanding of our life. When we yearn for sobriety and recovery, it may seem that our higher power is further than ever. Defeating addiction is by no means an instant miracle.

Mindfulness allows us a chance to learn and experience another component, and that is spirituality. Mindfulness brings us a stronger connection to our higher power and our spiritual practice. Even though prayer is possible at any time or place, whether loud, quiet, isolated, or crowded, it's taking the time to get in touch with our higher power that's important. We can't reach a successful level of meditation and prayer without developing mindfulness skills.

Loving kindness

You may ask, "If this is a selfless practice, why am I focusing on myself?" Because you are not an isolated feature of the universe. You deserve loving kindness as anything else or anyone else.

As you make peace with your place in the universe, always remember that you are a worthy part of it. Your loving kindness can be neither loving nor kind if it does not include yourself. But don't worry if you're not there yet! The loving kindness you are capable of isn't limited to yourself, either. Its flow is an eternal one, always there, ready for you.

Loving kindness meditation is a popular self-care technique that boosts wellbeing and reduces stress. Those who regularly practice it can increase their capacity for forgiveness, connection to others, self-acceptance, and more.

This technique might be difficult at first. As you practice, you're asking yourself to send kindness out to others or back toward yourself. It may take a bit of practice to be open to receiving love. The people in your life love you just as you are. As you take this in, try to hold the feeling without rejecting it. Instead, allow yourself to bask in the warmth of these feelings.

Loving kindness meditation practice begins with noticing and recalling positive qualities in yourself. An excellent place to start is with pleasant memories from times you helped or supported others out of the goodness of your heart. Hold one or a few of these instances in mind, and allow feelings of joy and compassion to arise within you.

Next, silently recite phrases like personal hopes or intentions that will guide you through this exercise. Some standard terms include "May I be healthy, may I be happy, may I be safe, may I be free," and so on. Find phrases that resonate with you. Start to repeat the phrases in a comfortable rhythm, either in your head, or in a near-silent whisper. Hold your attention. When your attention wanders, return to your breath.

After focusing on the phrases, visualize yourself surrounded by a circle of people you admire for their kindness, love, warmth, or compassion. Envision yourself as the center of their attention, receiving their love, and continue repeating your phrases.

After some more time, return to the phrases. Release the visualization gently. As you continue to repeat these phrases, you effectively rewrite your relationship with yourself, moving from a place of hurt and sabotage to one of respect, trust, and kindness. When you get comfortable, try to radiate loving kindness to another individual. Hold them in your mind, recite "May so-and-so be healthy/happy/safe," or what it is you wish for them.

ACTIVITY: LOVING KINDNESS MEDITATION AND REFLECTION

Write down *two* phrases of personal hope that resonate with you.

. . . .

. . . .

Write down *two* phrases that you would like to direct toward another person.

. . . .

. . . .

After meditating, reflect on how the practice felt.

. . . .

. . . .

What was the level of difficulty of doing this activity?

Easy | Moderate | Challenging | Difficult

How would you like to adapt this practice for your daily life?

. . . .

. . . .

Putting it all together

In examining Step Eleven, we discussed the motivations behind keeping a spiritual practice and considered what prayer could look like in our lives. Further, maintaining consistent mindfulness is a primary way to accumulate positive emotions. Here, the goal is to partake in enjoyable and satisfying experiences each day, thereby accumulating positive emotions in the short term, and preventing unpleasant feelings from becoming overwhelming. Prioritizing your wellbeing is necessary for developing a healthy self-image and relationship with yourself. This is done through mindfulness, or being in the present moment where we have control, and honing the ability to balance our emotional responses and actions in turn.

When we add meditation practice, this elevates our awareness inward, and we recognize a more significant potential for love toward ourselves and others. A spiritual approach may include prayer, but finding and keeping faith can be what you make it. Cultivating a connection with your higher power gives you confidence and guidance along your journey of personal growth.

By permitting ourselves to experience self-love and kindness, we also expand our capacity to feel this kindness toward others. Holding ourselves in the same esteem as we do all beings can bring a new level of peace and security, and reminds us what's important.

Chapter 12

Step Twelve: Carry the Message and Practice the Principles

In this chapter:
→ Stage 4 of DBT
   - Activity: Step Twelve
→ Core mindfulness skills: WHAT and HOW
   - Activity: Practicing non-judgmentalness
   - Activity: Practicing one-mindfulness
   - Activity: Diary card
→ Observing your feelings

Step Twelve	The DBT translation
Step Twelve is about sharing your experience, strength, and hope by staying active in service one day at a time	Using the core mindfulness skills in DBT, we can set intentions and turn the practice of commitment and being of service into a value

Stage 4 of DBT

Stage 4 of DBT focuses on achieving transcendence and building capacity for joy. In working Steps Ten, Eleven, and Twelve, you are encouraged to take an honest look at yourself, promptly admit you are wrong, and rebuild your true self, little by little. These align with the Steps worked in Stage 4.

Targets of Stage 4 of DBT

Types of meditation	Target
Mindfulness meditation Spiritual meditation Focus meditation Movement meditation Mantra meditation Transcendental meditation Progressive relaxation Loving kindness meditation Visualization meditation	Deeper meaning through spiritual existence

Today I am grateful for my alcoholism and bipolar disorder. Not only can I see how it brought me to an early bottom, but it also keeps me from getting complacent. Because I am vulnerable mentally and emotionally, I cannot afford to rest on my laurels. Having bipolar disorder has also afforded me the experience to understand and help others who struggle with mental illness in addition to alcoholism/addiction—yet another example of how our dark past can become our greatest asset! My service to others continues to help me get out of myself. Recovery is, for me, much greater than not drinking or abusing other drugs. It's a process I started as a teenager, and I have grown mentally, emotionally, physically, and spiritually. Therapy in its various forms, Twelve-Step meetings, getting help and support from others, and service work have been the center of my ongoing sobriety, healing, change, and growth.

The second part of Step Twelve is about carrying the message of recovery to other people. This is because, as the saying goes, "You can't keep it unless you give it away." When we work with others, our lives change.

The Twelve Steps is a program of attraction, not promotion. We lead by our own example, so talk to people when they reach out and when the time is right. They'll ask: "How can I get what you've got?" Focus your message on what it was like, what happened, and what it's like now. When talking to a newcomer, let go of labels. Tell your story truthfully, and let other people decide if it rings true for them.

Sometimes carrying the message can be as simple as making sure that there is a warm, caring, non-judgmental place for other alcoholics or addicts to come for a handshake or a hug that says, "We're here for you—come on in—and keep coming back!"

The beauty of Step Twelve is part of many promises of working the AA/NA program. Life takes on new meaning: watching people recover, helping others, and noticing loneliness vanish. Frequent contact with newcomers, and each other, is the bright spot of our new lives.

⊕ ACTIVITY: STEP TWELVE

How do you use your relationship with your higher power to make the world a better place?

. . . .

. . . .

Have you reached out to a recovering addict or an addict in pain?

. . . .

. . . .

What kind of support would you have liked to receive when you started the program?

. . . .

. . . .

How did you handle conflict before starting recovery? Has working the Steps changed that? If so, how?

. . . .

. . . .

How are you of service to the fellowship and other addicts?

. . . .

. . . .

Do you think you are ready to be a sponsor? If not, what do you think you need to work on to get to that stage?

. . . .

. . . .

Having understood the principles of recovery how do you plan to apply these in your daily life?

. . . .

. . . .

We are not promised tomorrow. To move forward with purpose and courage, take things day by day. Practicing mindfulness can be vital to feeling capable and ready to handle our feelings and responses to any situation. The following skills are an in-depth version of the mindfulness concepts explored previously. Becoming familiar with these techniques helps us maintain emotional stability.

Core mindfulness skills: WHAT and HOW

"Mindfulness" is a way of describing the act of "seeing the small things at the moment." Focusing on the current moment and being in it helps prevent you from agonizing over the past or future-tripping. It is not easy to do, as controlling your mind can often be challenging. So how do we do it? Simply put, the "WHAT" skills teach you to observe, describe, and participate, and the "HOW" skills teach you *how* to observe, describe, and participate.[40] These skills can be valuable tools to acquire and practice to still the mind and focus.

WHAT skills

The act of observing how others are coping and how we can be of service to them, describing our story to a newcomer, participating in meetings, and being of service more broadly—the principles of Step Twelve—are similar to the "WHAT" skills of DBT—observe, describe, and participate.

As we know, mindfulness is a core concept in DBT, where we work on developing a conscious awareness of ourselves and our surroundings. Practicing the following skills becomes a habit. Start with the "WHAT" skills, and work your way up to mastering mindfulness. A daily routine can help you develop a structure and helps you feel more in control of your emotions. Practicing mindfulness skills has many advantages, including improved emotion regulation, flexibility, empathy, and decreased stress and anxiety, to name a few.

- *Observe:* Right now, what is happening in your environment and around you? What sensations, feelings, and thoughts are you experiencing? Notice your emotions, but avoid being judgmental about them. Notice your thought processes, but don't label them "good" or "bad." On the other hand, do not push anything away—be open to all of your thoughts, observations, and feelings as they emerge. Use your five senses—eyesight, hearing, sense of touch, taste, and smell—to improve your observation skills.
- *Describe:* Use words to describe your experience. It can be helpful to say your descriptions out loud. For example, "I am aware that I feel anxious." "I am aware that my body is shivering after swimming in Berkeley Marina." "I am aware that my heart rate is slowing down." Be mindful not to attach any labels or judgments to what you are describing.
- *Participate:* Practice immersing yourself into each experience—stay in the "NOW." Integrate your "observe" and "describe" skills into what you are doing. For example, let's say one of your hobbies is practicing an instrument. Practice without any distractions. Allow yourself to be open to each experience once again without judging expectations or labels. Practice having a "Teflon mind"—let go of any negative or self-critical thoughts.

For instance, when I'm practicing guitar, sometimes I think I'll never get this song right. Why bother? Instead, I now consciously reframe this line of thought. As long as I keep practicing, I will improve. Enjoying the experience of making music is why I love playing guitar in the first place. Bring yourself back to the present task with self-kindness, and hold an appreciation for the moment you're in right now.

HOW skills
"HOW" skills teach you *how* to observe, describe, and participate.[41]

- *Nonjudgmentally:* Why is it essential to release judgments? First, let go of conclusions you have about yourself (e.g., "I can't do anything right") and others (e.g., "They can't get anything right"). Judgments increase our emotional pain and hurt relationships.
    Dragnet was a TV show about two Los Angeles police detectives. Sergeant Joe Friday was masterful at separating opinions, interpretations, and biases from the facts. His trademark statement was "just the facts." Friday would insert "just the facts" when he realized witnesses were starting to share opinions and judgments. Separating fact from fiction, he effectively got to the truth.[42]

Say, for example, your partner still isn't home and hasn't called. You might think, "She's so selfish. She doesn't respect me enough to call. It's time to reactivate my Bumble account." Being judgmental makes you miserable. "Just the facts" takes judgment and blame out of the equation. For instance, "I'm worried that she hasn't let me know. I would appreciate at least a text to know she is okay."

It's often not easy, but how do you let go of judgments? Start by letting go of the notion that every situation is either black or white or good or evil. Instead, observe and assess the facts logically. For example, perhaps you overvalue someone and think they're the most incredible person in the world. But when they do something that you don't like or agree with, it is easy to believe in absolutes and undervalue them—assuming they are the worst.

Similarly, it is not effective to judge yourself. This might be the harshest form of criticism and often the hardest thing to let go. We're human, and judging ourselves and others is so ingrained in us, it's second nature. When you are nonjudgmental, you radically accept yourself just the way you are. This approach does not imply that you are opposed to making changes, but you learn to separate the facts from judgment. For example, you can reframe your thinking by saying, "I have trouble sometimes being productive," instead of saying, "I'm worthless."

- *One-mindfully:* This means the act of focusing your mind on one thing at a time. In AA/NA, we focus on "one day at a time," sometimes "one minute at a time." Do one thing at a time. When you are driving, drive (don't text *and* drive); when you are conversing with someone, focus on the conversation. Most of us multitask, which means we are not focused on the task at hand. By taking each one at a time with one-mindfulness, we strengthen our skills. Let go of distractions and go back to what you were doing, again and again. Concentrate. If you find yourself doing two things at once, stop and go back to one thing at a time. Meditation is a one-mindful practice that allows us to focus our minds and let go of interruptions. During our day, we can act effectively by completing the task at hand without pausing to check our texts, answer emails, and think of the next job on our to-do list. We can choose to play volleyball, write a song, talk on the phone, or walk in nature by being focused right here, right now.

- *Effectively:* Be aware of when we are practicing mindfulness, learning, and sharpening our practice. Being effective means that we progress and strengthen our skills the more we practice mindfulness. Focus on what works. Do what needs to be done in each situation to meet your larger goals. Steer clear of "right and wrong." Act as skillfully as you can, meeting the needs of the problem you are in, not the situation you wish you were in. Out of awareness, we become more aware of the "pause" between our thoughts and actions. We extend the "pause"—a valuable skill for alcoholics and addicts. Becoming skillful at the practice of mindfulness enhances our ability to reduce our judgment of others. Being effective helps us let go of emotions that hurt us and develop our sense of compassion. When we practice effectively, we reinforce this mindfulness skill. Practicing effectively means we suffer less pain on our path to recovery.

⊕ ACTIVITY: PRACTICING NON-JUDGMENTALNESS

1. Identify a negative judgment about yourself, someone else, or a situation.

. . . .

. . . .

. . . .

2. Describe the advantages of letting go of this judgment.

. . . .

. . . .

. . . .

3. Describe the judgment factually.

. . . .

. . . .

. . . .

4. What is the mindful form of that judgment? (State the facts and how you feel.)

. . . .

· ·

· ·

ACTIVITY: PRACTICING ONE-MINDFULNESS

Start by planning to act one-mindfully this week. For example, focus entirely on one meal without any distractions from watching TV or checking your phone. Do the dishes and concentrate fully on the task while doing so. Or even go outside for a walk without listening to music. Aim to do one thing at a time by being present.

List *three* activities you plan to do:

1. ·

2. ·

3. ·

Once you have completed your activities, reflect on them. Write down how you felt doing one thing at a time. What were your challenges and distractions? Did you enjoy yourself more doing one thing at a time?

Activity 1:

· ·

· ·

· ·

· ·

· ·

· ·

What was the level of difficulty of doing this activity one-mindfully?

Easy | Moderate | Challenging | Difficult

Activity 2:

. . . .

. . . .

. . . .

. . . .

. . . .

. . . .

What was the level of difficulty of doing this activity one-mindfully?

Easy | Moderate | Challenging | Difficult

Activity 3:

. . . .

. . . .

. . . .

. . . .

. . . .

. . . .

What was the level of difficulty of doing this activity one-mindfully?

Easy | Moderate | Challenging | Difficult

ACTIVITY: DIARY CARD

This activity is taken from an interview with psychologist Dr Keith Sutton, who developed this custom diary card.[43]

How to use this card

Write down *three* problems and *five* emotions. Track your urges and actions and your unhealthy coping mechanisms—self-harm, suicidal ideation, drug and alcohol abuse, rage, avoidance, urge to go on social media. The goal is to track the relationship between the emotions and forms of coping.

On the back side of the card, write down things that have worked for you in the past to help you cope with urges: walking your dog, talking to friends, going for a hike, etc. The coping skills you list on the back are like a menu. For example: when you feel the urge to drink, you decide to walk the dog instead, which means your dog may get a lot of exercise at first! Another suggestion is that when you feel the urge to engage in destructive behaviors, try leaving the situation, doing something active like pushups or deep breathing. While breathing may help calm you down, sometimes you need to expel your energy, like jogging around the block or taking a cold shower.

After finishing these activities, go back to the card and rate on a scale of 1 to 10 your urge to drink or take drugs.

It's important now to document whether you acted on this urge: yes or no?

Rate your emotions—for example, anger, shame, depression, and happiness—on a scale of 1–10.

In response to feeling these emotions, e.g., anger, what coping skill on the list did you use? Put a checkmark next to it. For example: walking the dog, talking to a friend.

If you don't have a therapist to review this diary card with you each week, take the time to review the card on your own on a weekly basis to track your progress.

The use of this diary card is to help you get in touch with experiencing the urge and gaining mindfulness of your actions instead of just reacting. The goal of practicing these skills is to gain tolerance of your feelings. Sometimes just the observation of our behaviors is enough to start making a change. Research has shown that just tracking these behaviors can help bring about change because you are more aware of them.

Some tips to help remember to fill out this card

Add a reminder on your phone, keep it next to your bed, or tape the card to the back of your door.

Example diary card: Front

Name		M	Tu	W	Th	F	Sa	Su
Problem: Marijuana	Urge							
	Action							
Problem: Rage	Urge							
	Action							
Problem: Avoidance	Urge							
	Action							
Emotion: Anger								
Emotion: Shame								
Emotion: Depressed								
Emotion: Happiness								

Example diary card: Back

Name	M	Tu	W	Th	F	Sa	Su
Walking dog							
Talking to a friend							
CBT thought record							
Deep breathing							
Exercise							

Observing your feelings

Everybody has their own bodily signals indicating current, on-the-spot feelings. In other words, almost all emotions have some sort of physical reaction to them. Being aware of your physical reactions can help you better understand what emotion you may be feeling.[44] Below are some common physical symptoms for different emotions:

Physical symptom: tight muscles, clenched fists.
Emotions: mad, angry, frustrated, spiteful, jealous.

Physical symptom: smiling.
Emotions: happy, content, pleased, good-humored, excited, proud, confident.

Physical symptom: frowning.
Emotions: upset, sad, mad, disappointed.

Physical symptom: weakness.
Emotions: tired, depressed, hopeless.

Physical symptom: crying.
Emotions: sad, depressed, exhausted, upset, joyful.

Physical symptom: lowered head.
Emotions: shy, embarrassed, depressed, disgusted, ashamed.

Physical symptom: sweating.
Emotions: anxious, scared, worried.

Physical symptom: speechless.
Emotions: shocked, surprised.

Physical symptom: blushing.
Emotions: embarrassed, shy, guilty, ashamed.

Physical symptom: "in a fog."
Emotions: overwhelmed, worried, confused.

For instance, when I am overly stressed or concerned, I tend to bounce my leg or clench my jaw. Often, I don't consciously realize I'm feeling stressed until I catch myself in the act. Then I take a moment to unclench, relax my muscles, and reset. I can then ask myself, "What exactly is causing my stress right now? Is the present situation or task worth the intensity of such feelings? How can I adjust so I feel calmer and in a better state to handle the present situation?"

Think back over the last week or two. What were some of your physical reactions to various emotions? Personalize these symptoms by adding to them or changing them as needed. You may want to ask close family and friends since they may be aware of particular reactions you're not aware of.

Physical symptom: . . . .

Emotions: . . . .

Physical symptom: . . . .

Emotions: . . . .

Physical symptom: . . . .

Emotions: . . . .

Putting it all together

In Step Twelve we acknowledged our commitment to support others who are in recovery from addiction. An important part of our recovery occurs when we help other people. When we lead by example, our lives change. Step Twelve helps us make plans to reach out to others, offering our time and wisdom having gone through the Twelve Steps ourselves.

As we reached Stage 4 of DBT, which focuses on expanding our capacity for joy, we moved closer to realizing a state of transcendence. We also learned different types of mindfulness skills, including core mindfulness skills—the HOW and WHAT skills. With practice, you will be able to hold an awareness of our experiences without it leading us toward negative thought patterns. Mindfulness skills support us to remain anchored and less easily affected by our judgmental, emotional mind.

Using a diary card helps track our unhealthy coping behaviors. By keeping track of the relationship between our emotions and certain actions, we can undo the tethers that keep us bound to habits we want to break. Using this method, we replace an unhealthy activity with a healthy one. Honing our ability to remain present also prevents us from agonizing over the past or future. A helpful method for breaking this down is focusing on doing just "one thing at a time."

Conclusion

A Life Worth Living Beyond Your Wildest Dreams

I began my recovery when I was not yet an adult, therefore it took me longer to grasp an understanding of myself and the struggles I faced. Regardless of where we begin, each one of us has the potential to change our lives and make them worth living.

Through AA, I found other people like me. The Twelve Steps became a guide that brought me through the depths of my struggles—from the lowest parts of the valley out to the other side. By acknowledging the truth of my addiction and my powerlessness, I started to disentangle myself from its influence over every part of my life. Now I can bask in the sunlight of healthy self-love and the love of others that I once thought didn't exist.

At first, overcoming the addict mind and thought distortions were huge hurdles. I couldn't trust myself nor recognize what it was I was truly fighting. My brain told me I wasn't good enough, making it seem impossible to mend the relationship with myself. Avoidance seemed like the better option, but I recognized that the power to change is within us and only us. More than that, your higher power and mine want only to inform, guide, and accompany us at each Step.

My first leap of faith was through Radical Acceptance, something that felt impossible reflecting on my shortcomings. For many of us, self-acceptance does not come naturally in any capacity and must be set as an intention. I acknowledged my problems and harmful behaviors. Then I began to practice accepting myself wholly and willingly, with kindness and sympathy, as I would my most cherished friend. Through self-compassion, I gave myself loving permission to change. This shift in mindset made it possible to consider different outcomes than I had before. I spoke to my higher power regularly. Soon, I felt my potential grow: I yearned to find a life that mattered, a life through which meaning flowed.

However, I sometimes still feel stuck. When faced with difficult circumstances, my emotions can overshadow my progress. They're too big, too loud, too overwhelming, when I am operating from an Emotion Mind—and in overdrive. The HOW and WHAT skills from DBT guided me in effectively using the right tools to address difficult situations. Over time, I learned to balance my Emotion Mind by applying my Reasonable Mind, the logical state of mind used to accomplish concrete tasks. The result is a Wise Mind, a middle ground where I could hold both my feelings and emotions and act from a place of informed, logical self-awareness. There was nothing "wrong" with me; I merely didn't have the skills I needed to help me do it differently.

AA showed me I would never get there if I held on to the need to maintain control. I turned my life and will over, asked for help, and allowed myself to be held and healed. Even with my higher power at my side, my interpersonal relationships were still rocky. I found it challenging to balance my needs with others'. With daily practice, interpersonal effectiveness skills gave me the structure to establish healthy boundaries, fulfill my needs and desires, and maintain healthy relationships. Sometimes, the right thing to do was to walk away; at other times, clear and honest communication paved the way for healing and reconciliation.

I still sometimes have bad days when the negatives in life outweigh the positives, making me question everything. To offset the bad, I work on planning out good things to look forward to each day, actively accumulating positives in my life to keep a balanced emotional state. But recovery is a process, not an event. The activities both help my mood and do something with my life that resonates with my values.

But before leaping wholly into a new life determined by my values, I needed to make a personal inventory of those in my life I'd harmed. After admitting my mistakes to my higher power, I worked up the courage to share my mistakes with my sponsor. While working on my Step Four inventory, I got a new perspective on the bigger picture of my patterns in most situations. This wisdom further strengthened my commitment to sobriety.

The community and the friends I found in AA offered me support, company, and the confidence to admit my faults. They affirmed my innate value and the strength of my efforts. This hope pushed me forward. I learned to be more assertive yet gentle; through consistent practice applying interpersonal effectiveness skills, it became possible to lower my emotional reactivity in intense situations.

An important next step in my recovery was continual mindfulness practice. By prioritizing my awareness of the present moment and withholding judgment, my decision-making abilities improved as I drew on both reason and emotion when formulating a response.

When I reached Step Seven, entrusting my higher power was only half the equation; the other half was about taking personal responsibility for my behavior. For me, this Step hinged on learning to hold a balanced view of any situation. To walk the middle path simultaneously validates myself and others.

Something was still missing. I needed to understand how best to approach conflict versus how I was used to approaching it. Using the DBT skill of building mastery, I learned to be aware of my personal goals before entering a conflict scenario or discussion, and how to route those plans into action through effective and gentle communication. I started to notice that I was building competency at these skills! The bulk of my growing toolkit continued to boost my confidence and self-esteem.

Step Nine is about being free. But before I could taste that freedom, I had amends to make. In this case, the only way out is through. I knew that not everyone I had harmed would be keen to receive my amends. For their sake and mine, I knew it was important to lay the groundwork not to make the same mistakes. For this, I drew on the Cope Ahead skill. This helped me to identify problematic patterns of interactions that I was prone to. Analyzing these patterns helped interrupt the cycle of destructive behaviors before they could repeat.

However, I still felt vulnerable. At times, I noticed that I was on the receiving end of emotional invalidation: my emotions were minimized, doubted, or dismissed. To guard against feelings of invalidation, I learned to initiate effective communication by listening actively and validating others. This way, I know I did the best I could do. In these situations, the skills of recovering from invalidation can help. Although at times it is tough, always remember to practice self-compassion.

Next, I turned to Step Ten. As I continued to take a personal inventory, I found it helpful to use DBT chain analysis to identify the causes of past hurts and, with practice, to increase my tolerance to distress. Using the opposite action skill also encourages us to reflect on specific triggers or instances of hurt, dealt by ourselves as well as others. We can then identify the potentials for implementing a constructive response instead. The more I put all these skills together in my life, the more I noticed that I felt lighter. It was becoming easier to maintain my honesty, integrity, and self-discipline.

At times, despite these tools, unpleasant feelings were overwhelming and I didn't know what to do. I knew I needed to improve my wellbeing in another way. Although difficult at first, I started a meditation practice, giving myself space to calm my mind and reach inward. My spiritual approach came to include both meditation and prayer. Asking for help is one of the most powerful tools we have. Trusting in my higher power helped keep me anchored as I reconnected with the core of my being. With meditation, I began to recognize my potential for deep loving kindness toward myself and others. I found my place as equal and equally deserving among all beings. At Step Twelve, I reflected on all I had gone through to get here. It wasn't easy. And it sure wasn't quick! It was time to give back what I had learned, both in AA and with DBT—sticking to my values and walking my talk. I helped others learn how using DBT skills could enhance their recovery too.

Then I decided to put everything together—all the experience and expertise I've acquired—into creating this workbook. This book is specifically designed to help other people with problems similar to those I faced. My intention for you is that instead of feeling isolated, alone, and without hope of changing, my story can serve as a template, an inspiration, and a realistic model for recovering from addiction or alcoholism alongside mental health difficulties. At the same time, it gave me purpose to serve the broader community of others working through the (at times arduous and demanding) process of recovery, an extension of my Step Twelve.

I felt the need to speak to the intersection of people, like me, whose mental health challenges are part of life alongside the challenges of being a recovering alcoholic and addict. Taking prescribed medication to manage mental health is not mutually exclusive with the Twelve Steps. However, some people will still not consider you clean and sober if you take prescribed medications. (I would strongly encourage these individuals to read the pamphlet "The AA Member—Medications and Other Drugs.")

I'm here as an example that it is worth it to complete the Twelve Steps and push on in your recovery despite setbacks. Ignore those who may attempt to sabotage or doubt you. Instead, keep in mind: improvement is almost never linear, but it is absolutely reachable! With the tools and activities I've collected here, you can always go back to an activity again or utilize a technique in a new setting. You could stick colorful tabs in places you want to reference frequently.

As we disentangle the web of harmful patterns, thoughts, and habits, we turn back to our genuine selves. We may be scared at first, rediscovering ourselves anew—and that is perfectly okay! There is nothing wrong with reinventing yourself at any point in life, in recovery from addiction or otherwise. We never graduate from the Twelve-Step program. Just like we, ourselves, never "graduate" from growing, learning, relearning, and growing some more—again, and again, and again.

You, me, all of us have innate value and a unique set of offerings to the world. Let patience, compassion, and mindfulness hold that spark of self-love for you. Nurture it, check in on it, and when you are ready, share it far and wide.

Acknowledgments

It takes a village to help someone recover from mental illness and alcoholism. I want to thank my fellow DBT group members, Rob, Sarah, Morgan, and Kerry, at Kaiser Permanente, and DBT individual therapist, Dr William Selig. A special thanks to group leaders Veronica Ochoa, LCSW, and Sabrina Chaumette, LCSW, for your expertise, guidance, and support.

My eternal gratitude to Kennedy Cosgrove, MD, Psychiatrist, Kaiser Permanente. Thank you for being there, listening without judgment, and advocating on my behalf.

Thank you to the AA/NA community, especially the folks at the 9am El Cerrito Fellowship Daily Open Speaker/Discussion Meeting, the Monday 7:15pm LGBTQ Living in the Solution, and the Saturday 9am Rockridge Fellowship Sane and Sober Meeting, WM, Trans, GQ. You offered me hope and held me with care, love, and support as I walked through my despair, hopelessness, and grief one day at a time.

For Tina: your friendship, love, and daily phone calls gave me a soft place to land.

For April Topfer, thank you for your friendship, support, and having me join you at yoga class. Your unconditional love was a balm for my soul.

For Tonya, thank you for your friendship and service by initiating the Saturday morning Sane and Sober AA meeting.

To Keith, thank you for your support, love, and our weekly sponsorship dinner meetings.

For Alicia, thank you for your unconditional regard, love, and listening ear. Also, thank you for your phone calls and checking in.

I especially want to thank my younger sister, Celia van Maarth, for taking the time to listen, pray with me, and remind me of God's unconditional love and care.

Thank you to my older sister, Therese Haber, and brother-in-law, Jeff Haber, for sharing your stories and wisdom during our late-night talks. Thank you both for inviting me to spend the holidays, listening with open hearts, and feeding me well!

I couldn't have done it without support from my father, Francis "Pete" Petracek (RIP). Your weekly Sunday afternoon calls shored me up with love and support. I miss you and love you.

My dear friend Rhonda Williamson, for your hearty laugh, jokes, and friendship.

Bea Depuydt. Your friendship, steady presence, encouraging texts, and phone calls helped me keep going.

Kate Raphael. My beloved friend, thank you for standing by me all these years. And thank you for sharing your delicious culinary skills!

A special thank you to Helene, my BFF in recovery—our journey together started 42 years ago. I'm so grateful for your consistent love, compassion, caring, stream of postcards, and loving phone calls.

Michelle (RIP), thank you for being a dear, loving, kind friend. You were there when I needed you. You always cheered me up when I was down. You came over to my house when I was lonely. You sat with me many times, listening. I will never forget your smile and unconditional love.

I am eternally grateful to Margot Yvette Reed. Thank you for your understanding, patience, late-night phone calls, and for always being the person I could turn to during those dark and desperate times.

To David Allen Fisher, LMFT. Your support, care, and guidance were a shining light for my soul. Thank you for saving mine.

וכל־המקיים נפש אחת מעלין עליו כאילו קיים קיים עולם מלא

Whoever saves one life saves the world.

I owe a debt of gratitude to those who have supported this project from the beginning. My early readers were a sounding board that kept me on track. To Kate Raphael, for your enthusiasm and "go for it" attitude; Elaine Beale, for your keen eye; Diana Shapiro, for your willingness to read a Step and suggest changes; Binah Bean, for your support, friendship, and sharing of our mutual path; and Eric Lyden, for your desire to read first drafts and offer hope.

To my editor extraordinaire, Mikaela Barad, for jumping into this project with both feet at the 11th hour! Thank you for your eagerness to take on this project and power through.

Writing a book about my life and recovery was a surreal process. It was harder than I thought and more rewarding than I imagined. None of this would have been possible without my dear friend, housemate, and pandemic bubble buddy, Snigdha Pamula. You have stood by me during every struggle and success in writing this book. Your laughter, inquiring mind, and shared meals and walks enabled me to bring this book to fruition. This book is as much yours as it is mine.

With gratitude and endless thanks to the doctors, nurses, and staff at the ICU unit at Fairview Hospital, Minneapolis, for saving my life on that dark night many years ago. Also, heartfelt thanks to the psychiatric staff and Fairview Adolescent Unit for your patience, support, and love.

And finally, thank you, God, for giving me a second chance. Thank you for giving me the strength to keep going. Thank you for the loving family, friends, and community that surrounds me. Thank you for walking with me, for it is by faith, not by sight, that you have guided me. Thank you, God, for the breath of life and hope. All in all, thank you God, for *everything*.

For more information on my private practice and other services, go to: www.laurapetracekphd.com

Endnotes

1   Linehan, M. M. (1993). *Skills Training Manual for Treating Borderline Personality Disorder*. New York: Guilford Press.

2   Linehan, M. M., Schmidt, H., Dimeff, L. A., Craft, J. C., Kanter, J., & Comtois, K. A. (1999). Dialectical behavior therapy for patients with borderline personality disorder and drug-dependence. *American Journal on Addictions 8*(4), 279–292, doi:10.1080/105504999305686.

3   Dimeff, L. A. & Linehan, M. M. (2008). Dialectical behavior therapy for substance abusers. *Addiction Science & Clinical Practice 4*(2), 39–47, doi:10.1151/ascp084239; Stotts, A. L. & Northrup, T. F. (2015). The promise of third-wave behavioral therapies in the treatment of substance use disorders. *Current Opinion in Psychology 2*, 75–81, doi:10.1016/j.copsyc.2014.12.028; Cavicchioli, M., Movalli, M., Vassena, G., Ramella, P., Prudenziati, F., & Maffei, C. (2019). The therapeutic role of emotion regulation and coping strategies during a stand-alone DBT skills training program for alcohol use disorder and concurrent substance use disorders. *Addictive Behaviors 98*, 106035. https://doi.org/10.1016/j.addbeh.2019.106035; Haktanır, A. & Callender, K. A. (2020). Meta-analysis of dialectical behavior therapy (DBT) for treating substance use. *Research on Education and Psychology*, Systematic Reviews and Meta Analysis, Special Issue, 4, 74–87.

4   Linehan, M. M. (2015). *DBT Skills Training Manual* (Second edn). New York: Guilford Press.

5   Bolte-Taylor, J. (2009). *My Stroke of Insight: A Brain Scientist's Personal Journey*. London: Hodder & Stoughton.

6   Linehan, M. M. (1993). *Skills Training Manual for Treating Borderline Personality Disorder*. New York: Guilford Press.

7   Linehan, M. M. (1993). *Skills Training Manual for Treating Borderline Personality Disorder*. New York: Guilford Press.

8   Linehan, M. M. (1993). *Skills Training Manual for Treating Borderline Personality Disorder*. New York: Guilford Press.

9   Linehan, M. M. (1993). *Cognitive Behavioral Therapy of Borderline Personality Disorder*. New York: Guilford Press.

10   Linehan, M. M. (1993). *Skills Training Manual for Treating Borderline Personality Disorder*. New York: Guilford Press.

11   Dimeff, L. A. & Linehan, M. M. (2008). Dialectical behavior therapy for substance abusers. *Addiction Science & Clinical Practice 4*(2), 39–47, doi:10.1151/ascp084239.

12   McCrady, B. S. (1994). Alcoholics Anonymous and behavior therapy: Can habits be treated as diseases? Can diseases be treated as habits? *Journal of Consulting and Clinical Psychology 62*(6), 1159–1166. https://doi.org/10.1037/0022-006X.62.6.1159

13   Dimeff, L. A. & Linehan, M. M. (2008). Dialectical behavior therapy for substance abusers. *Addiction Science & Clinical Practice 4*(2), 39-47, doi:10.1151/ascp084239.

14   Linehan, M. M. (2015). *DBT Skills Training Manual* (Second edn). New York: Guilford Press.

15   Rogers, C. (2012). *On Becoming a Person: A Therapist's View of Psychotherapy*. Boston, MA: Houghton Mifflin Harcourt.

16 AA (Alcoholics Anonymous) (2001). *Alcoholics Anonymous Big Book* (4th edn). Alcoholics Anonymous World Services, p.45.

17 Linehan, M. M. (1993). *Skills Training Manual for Treating Borderline Personality Disorder*. New York: Guilford Press.

18 Linehan, M. M. (1993). *Skills Training Manual for Treating Borderline Personality Disorder*. New York: Guilford Press.

19 Deikman, A. (1982). *The Observing Self: Mysticism and Psychotherapy*. Lee's Summit, MO: Beacon Press.

20 Linehan, M. M. (1993). *Cognitive Behavioral Therapy of Borderline Personality Disorder*. New York: Guilford Press, p.214.

21 Lindberg Cedar, A. (2019). What is 'wise mind'?...and how it can help with you just about anything... Therapy for Real Life, February 10. https://medium.com/@therapybyannacedar/what-is-wise-mind-and-how-it-can-help-with-you-just-about-anything-d4b903479d24

22 AA (Alcoholics Anonymous) (2001). *Alcoholics Anonymous Big Book* (4th edn). Alcoholics Anonymous World Services, p.64.

23 Linehan, M. M. (1993). *Skills Training Manual for Treating Borderline Personality Disorder*. New York: Guilford Press.

24 AA (Alcoholics Anonymous) (2001). *Alcoholics Anonymous Big Book* (4th edn). Alcoholics Anonymous World Services, p.58.

25 Linehan, M. M. (1993). *Cognitive Behavioral Therapy of Borderline Personality Disorder*. New York: Guilford Press.

26 Brach, T. (2004). *Radical Acceptance: Embracing Your Life with the Heart of a Buddha*. New York: Bantam Books.

27 Gross, J. J. (1998). The emerging field of emotion regulation: An integrative review. *Review of General Psychology 2*, 271–299; Gross, J. J. (1999). Emotion regulation: Past, present, future. *Cognition and Emotion 13*(5), 551–573, doi:10.1080/026999399379186.

28 Wagner, A. W., Rizvi, S. L., & Harned, M. S. (2007). Applications of dialectical behavior therapy to the treatment of complex trauma-related problems: When one case formulation does not fit all. *Journal of Traumatic Stress 20*, 391–400.

29 Linehan, M. M. (2015). *DBT Skills Training Manual* (Second edn). New York: Guilford Press.

30 Linehan, M. M. (1993). *Skills Training Manual for Treating Borderline Personality Disorder*. New York: Guilford Press.

31 Chödrön, P. (2021). Nothing to (im)prove. *Tricycle: The Buddhist Review*, May 7. https://tricycle.org/trikedaily/pema-chodron-lovingkindness

32 Brach, T. (2004). *Radical Acceptance: Embracing Your Life with the Heart of a Buddha*. New York: Bantam Books.

33 Linehan, M. M. (1993). *Skills Training Manual for Treating Borderline Personality Disorder*. New York: Guilford Press.

34 Olivo, E. (2014). *Wise Mind Living: Master Your Emotions, Transform Your Life*. Boulder, CO: Sounds True.

35 Linehan, M. M. (2015). *DBT Skills Training Manual* (Second edn). New York: Guilford Press.

36 McKay, M., Wood, J. C., & Brantley, J. (2007). *The Dialectical Behavior Therapy Skills Workbook: Practical DBT Exercises for Learning Mindfulness, Interpersonal Effectiveness, Emotion Regulation, and Distress Tolerance*. Oakland, CA: New Harbinger Publications.

37 Rathus, J. H. & Miller, A. L. (2014). *DBT Skills Manual for Adolescents*. New York: Guilford Press. [Foreword by Marsha M. Linehan.]

38 Lamott, A. (2021). *Dusk, Night, Dawn: On Revival and Courage*. New York: Riverhead Books.

39 Linehan, M. M. (2015). *DBT Skills Training Manual* (Second edn). New York: Guilford Press.

40 Linehan, M. M. (2015). *DBT Skills Training Manual* (Second edn). New York: Guilford Press.

41 Linehan, M. M. (2015). *DBT Skills Training Manual* (Second edn). New York: Guilford Press.

42 Esmail, J. (2021). *DBT Metaphors and Stories*. Abingdon: Routledge.

43 Sutton, K. [Online interview]. (2021, April 12). www.drkeithsutton.com